PAUL AND HIS THEOLOGY

Rev. Albert F. Scariato, M.D.
3909 Albemarle Street, NW
Washington, DC 20016

PT 3-36 fr 1/23/01

PAUL AND HIS THEOLOGY

A Brief Sketch

SECOND EDITION

Joseph A. Fitzmyer, S.J.
Boston College

PRENTICE HALL
Upper Saddle River, New Jersey 07458

LIBRARY OF CONGRESS
Library of Congress Cataloging-in-Publication Data

Fitzmyer, Joseph A.
    Paul and his theology   a brief sketch / Joseph A. Fitzmyer   --
2nd ed.
        p.   cm.
    Rev ed. of· Pauline theology. a brief sketch. 1967.
    Bibliography· p.
    Includes index.
    ISBN 0-13-654419-3
    1 Bible. N.T Epistles of Paul--Theology.   I. Fitzmyer, Joseph
A. Pauline theology, a brief sketch. II. Title.
BS2651.F5 1989
227'.06--dc19   88-7274
                                                      CIP

Imprimi potest
V. Rev. James A. Devereux, S.J.
Provincial, Maryland Province of the Society of Jesus

Nihil obstat
Rev. Raymond E. Brown, S.S.
Censor Deputatus

Imprimatur
Rev. Msgr. Raymond J. Boland
Vicar General for the Archdiocese of Washington

May 7, 1987

The *nihil obstat* and *imprimatur* are official declarations that a book or pamphlet is free of doctrinal or moral error. No implication is contained therein that those who have granted the *nihil obstat* and the *imprimatur* agree with the content, opinions, or statements expressed.

Previous edition published under the title of PAULINE THEOLOGY:
A BRIEF SKETCH.

Editorial/production supervision and interior design: Virginia L. McCarthy
Cover design: Lundgren Graphics, Ltd.
Manufacturing buyer: Peter Havens

Printed in the United States of America
10 9 8 7 6 5 4

ISBN 0-13-654419-3

CONTENTS

Part Two: PAULINE THEOLOGY   23

Introduction   24

Dominant Perspectives   36

PREFACE

This book is a revision of my earlier work, *Pauline Theology: A Brief Sketch* (*PT*) (Prentice-Hall, Inc., 1967). As was true of *PT*, the text of this revision has been extracted from the larger forthcoming work, *The New Jerome Biblical Commentary* (*NJBC*) (eds. Raymond E. Brown, S.S.; Roland E. Murphy, O.Carm.; and Joseph A. Fitzmyer, S.J.) to be published by Prentice Hall in 1990. This extract is intended to alert readers to the coming *NJBC*, just as the original *PT* alerted the public to the coming of the *Jerome Biblical Commentary* (*JBC*). The success that the latter has enjoyed over the years since 1968 has encouraged the editors to launch a revised form of it. That success was attributable to the 50 contributors who wrote the 80 articles in the *JBC*. But scholarship must advance, and the editors of the *NJBC* are confident that they now have contributions that will better match the needs of the 1990s and the early twenty-first century. Consequently, we are happy to alert the public in this preliminary way to the coming of the *NJBC*.

As with the *JBC*, the *NJBC* will not be merely another "introduction" to the Bible, but a commentary on it in a true sense, that is, with comments on its verses. It will also include general articles, such as the two that comprise this book ("Paul" and "Pauline Theology"), intended to treat synthetically those subjects that the ordinary analytical comments on verses cannot adequately handle. The *NJBC* will be issued in one volume, with continuous pagination and improved runnings heads. The tone of the *NJBC* will be modern and will correspond to the development of Catholic biblical interpretation.

Like the commentary itself, this sketch about Paul and his theology is intended for students of the Bible—clerical, lay, and religious. It sets forth in compact form the dominant features of Paul's career and his teachings. Detailed explanations of Pauline passages are not presented here because they will be treated in the commentaries on individual letters in the *NJBC*. Rather, the aim of this text is that of a synthetic presentation of Paul and his theology in their broad outlines.

This revised sketch differs from the earlier form, however, in including an introductory part devoted to Paul himself: what can be reconstructed about his life and the order of his writings. The inspiration for the inclusion of this introductory part came from the Spanish translation of the brief sketch, in which what was called in the *JBC* "A Life of Paul" was included in *Teología de San Pablo: Síntesis y perspectivas* (Epifania 19; Madrid: Ediciones Cristiandad, 1975). Anyone who compares the Spanish translation of the sketch with the English original will realize that I had already begun at that time the revision of the sketch that is now presented in English in this new form.

The limited compass of this sketch results from its place in the *NJBC*. Cross references to other parts of the *NJBC* will be included in the form of the sketch to appear in the *NJBC* and they will supply some details omitted in the discussion here, but the cross references have had to be omitted in this preliminary form. The abbreviations used here are those that will be employed in the commentary itself. The marginal numerals correspond to those to be used in the *NJBC*.

Permission to use the table on pp. 3–5 has been graciously given by the author (Thomas H. Campbell) and by the editor of the *JBL* (V. P. Furnish). My thanks are due to both of these gentlemen.

Lastly, a word of gratitude has to be expressed to Raymond E. Brown, S.S., who is the editor of the general articles in the *NJBC;* his editorial comments have greatly improved the text of this brief sketch. Thanks too are also due to Mr. Joseph Heider, the religion editor of Prentice Hall, and to his staff, who have been responsible for seeing to the production of this book.

Joseph A. Fitzmyer, S.J.

Gasson Chair Professor, Department of Theology
Boston College
Chestnut Hill, MA 02167

ABBREVIATIONS

Abh.	Abhandlungen
Ag.Ap.	Josephus, *Against Apion*
AGJU	Arbeiten zur Geschichte des antiken Judentums und Urchristentums
ALBO	Analecta lovaniensia biblica et orientalia
AnBib	Analecta biblica
AnGreg	Analecta gregoriana
Ant.	Josephus, *Antiquities of the Jews*
Apoc. Mos.	*Apocalypse of Moses*
app. crit.	*apparatus criticus* (critical apparatus)
ARAB	D. D. Luckenbill (ed.), *Ancient Records of Assyria and Babylonia* (2 vols.; Chicago, 1926–27)
ASNU	Acta seminarii neotestamentici upsaliensis
ATR	*Anglican Theological Review*
BA	*Biblical Archaeologist*
BCH	*Bulletin de correspondance hellénique*
BEvT	Beiträge zur evangelischen Theologie
BHT	Beiträge zur historischen Theologie
Bib	*Biblica*
BJRL	*Bulletin of the John Rylands (University) Library (of Manchester)*
BR	*Biblical Research*
BSac	*Bibliotheca sacra*
BT	*The Bible Translator*
BTB	*Biblical Theology Bulletin*

BU	Biblische Untersuchungen
BZ	*Biblische Zeitschrift*
BZNW	Beiträge zur *ZNW*
CBQ	*Catholic Biblical Quarterly*
ChTSP	L. Cerfaux, *The Church in the Theology of Saint Paul* (NY, 1959)
CIL	*Corpus inscriptionum latinarum*
CJT	*Canadian Journal of Theology*
ClR	*Clergy Review*
ConBNT	Coniectanea biblica, New Testament
ConNT	Coniectanea neotestamentica
CSEL	Corpus scriptorum ecclesiasticorum latinorum
CTJ	*Calvin Theological Journal*
CTM	*Concordia Theological Monthly*
CurTM	*Currents in Theology and Mission*
DBSup	*Dictionnaire de la Bible Supplément*
Did.	*Didache* (*Teaching of the Twelve Apostles*)
DKP	K. Ziegler and W. Sontheimer (eds.), *Der kleine Pauly: Lexikon der Antike* (5 vols.; Stuttgart, 1964–75)
EB	*Enchiridion biblicum* (4th ed.; Naples, 1961)
EBib	Etudes bibliques
EKKNT	Evangelisch-katholischer Kommentar zum Neuen Testament
ENTT	E. Käsemann, *Essays on New Testament Themes* (SBT 41; London, 1964)
ESBNT	J. A. Fitzmyer, *Essays on the Semitic Background of the New Testament* (London, 1971; Missoula, MT 1974)
2 Esdr.	*Second Esdras* (one of the Apocrypha of the OT)
ETL	*Ephemerides theologicae lovanienses*
EvQ	*Evangelical Quarterly*
EvT	*Evangelische Theologie*
EWNT	H. Balz and G. Schneider (eds.), *Exegetisches Wörterbuch zum Neuen Testament* (3 vols.; Stuttgart, 1978–83)
ExpTim	*Expository Times*
FBBS	Facet Books, Biblical Series
Fest.	Festschrift (followed by the name of the person honored or remembered by the publication; used for books in any language)
frg.	fragment
FRLANT	Forschungen zur Religion und Literatur des Alten und Neuen Testaments
Gk	Greek (as an adjective)
GTA	Göttinger theologische Arbeiten

HALAT	W. Baumgartner et al., *Hebräisches und aramäisches Lexikon zum Alten Testament* (4 vols.; Leiden, 1967—)
HBC	J. Finegan, *Handbook of Biblical Chronology* (Princeton, 1964)
Hebr	Hebrew (as an adjective)
HJPAJC	E. Schürer, *The History of the Jewish People in the Age of Jesus Christ* (3 vols.; eds. G. Vermes and F. Miller; Edinburgh, 1973–87)
HR	*History of Religions*
HTR	*Harvard Theological Review*
HUT	Hermeneutische Untersuchungen zur Theologie
IDB	G. A. Buttrick (ed.), *The Interpreter's Dictionary of the Bible* (4 vols.; Nash, 1962)
IDBSup	*IDB* Supplementary Volume
Int	*Interpretation*
JAAR	*Journal of the American Academy of Religion*
JBL	*Journal of Biblical Literature*
JPST	*Journal of the Perkins School of Theology*
JTS	*Journal of Theological Studies*
Jub.	*The Book of Jubilees*
KD	*Kerygma und Dogma*
KJV	*King James Version*
LAE	A. Deissmann, *Light from the Ancient East* (2d ed.; London, 1927)
Lat	Latin (as an adjective)
LD	Lectio divina
LumVie	*Lumière et vie*
LXX	Septuagint (Greek Translation of OT)
MarThSt	Marburger theologische Studien
MT	Masoretic Text
MTS	Münchener theologische Studien
MUSJ	*Mélanges de l'Université Saint-Joseph*
N	North (direction of compass)
NIDNTT	C. Brown (ed.), *The New International Dictionary of New Testament Theology* (3 vols.; GR, 1975–78)
NovT	*Novum Testamentum*
NovTSup	Supplements to *NovT*
NRT	*La nouvelle revue théologique*
NT	New Testament
NTAbh	Neutestamentliche Abhandlungen
NTQT	E. Käsemann, *New Testament Questions of Today* (Phl, 1969)
NTS	*New Testament Studies*

OCD	N. G. L. Hammond and H. H. Scullard (eds.), *The Oxford Classical Dictionary* (2nd ed.; Oxford, 1970)
OT	Old Testament
OTNT	H. Conzelmann, *An Outline of the Theology of the New Testament* (NY, 1969)
Perspectives	E. Käsemann, *Perspectives on Paul* (Phl, 1971)
PG	J. Migne (ed.), Patrologia graeca
PW	G. Wissowa (ed.), *Paulys Real-Encyclopädie der klassischen Altertumswissenschaft* (Stuttgart, 1893—)
QD	Quaestiones disputatae
QL	Qumran Literature
RAM	*Revue d'ascétique et mystique*
RB	*Revue biblique*
RDTour	*Revue diocésaine de Tournai*
RechBib	Recherches bibliques
Rechtf	J. Friedrich et al. (eds.), *Rechtfertigung* (Fest. E. Käsemann; Tübingen, 1976)
Recueil	*Recueil Lucien Cerfaux* (3 vols.; Gembloux, 1964–72)
REG	*Revue des études grecques*
ResQ	*Restoration Quarterly*
RevQ	*Revue de Qumran*
RevScRel	*Revue des sciences religieuses*
RHPR	*Revue d'histoire et de philosophie religieuses*
RITNT	A. Richardson, *Introduction to the Theology of the New Testament* (London, 1958)
RivB	*Rivista biblica*
RSR	*Recherches de science religieuse*
RSV	*Revised Standard Version*
S	South (direction of the compass)
SANT	Studien zum Alten und Neuen Testament
SBLDS	Society of Biblical Literature Dissertation Series
SBM	Stuttgarter biblische Monographien
SBS	Stuttgarter biblische Studien
SBT	Studies in Biblical Theology
ScEs	Science et esprit
SE I, II, etc.	*Studia evangelica I, II, III*, etc. (= Texte und Untersuchungen 73, 87, 88, 102, 103, 112)
SEA	*Svensk exegetisk årsbok*
Sir	Sirach (or Ben Sira)
SJLA	Studies in Judaism in Late Antiquity
SJT	*Scottish Journal of Theology*
SNTSMS	Studiorum Novi Testamenti Societas Monograph Series

SPat	*Studia patavina*
SPC	*Studiorum paulinorum congressus internationalis catholicus 1961* (2 vols.; AnBib 17, 18; Rome, 1963)
TAG	J. A. Fitzmyer, *To Advance the Gospel* (NY, 1981)
TDNT	G. Kittel and G. Friedrich (eds.), *Theological Dictionary of the New Testament* (10 vols.; GR, 1964–76)
TEH	Theologische Existenz heute
TLZ	*Theologische Literaturzeitung*
TNT	R. Bultmann, *The Theology of the New Testament* (2 vols.; NY, 1952–55)
TRE	G. Krause and G. Müller (eds.), *Theologische Real-Enzyklopädie* (30 vols.; Berlin, 1973—)
TS	*Theological Studies*
TToday	*Theology Today*
TZ	*Theologische Zeitschrift*
UNT	Untersuchungen zum Neuen Testament
v, vv	verse, verses
US	*Una sancta*
VD	*Verbum domini*
VP	*Vivre et penser* (= *RB* 50–52 [1941–45])
WA	J. A. Fitzmyer, *A Wandering Aramean* (SBLMS 25; Missoula, MT, 1979)
Wis	Wisdom (of Solomon)
WF	Wege der Forschung
WMANT	Wissenschaftliche Monographien zum Alten und Neuen Testament
WUNT	Wissenschaftliche Untersuchungen zum Neuen Testament
ZNW	*Zeitschrift für die neutestamentliche Wissenschaft*
ZTK	*Zeitschrift für Theologie und Kirche*

Dead Sea Scrolls

1QH	Thanksgiving Psalms (*Hôdāyôt*) from Qumran Cave 1
1QM	War Scroll (*Milḥāmāh*) from Qumran Cave 1
1QpHab	Commentary (*pēšer*) on Habakkuk from Qumran Cave 1
1QS	Manual of Discipline (*Serek*) from Qumran Cave 1
4QEn^h	The Book of Enoch from Qumran Cave 4, copy b
4QFlor	Florilegium from Qumran Cave 4
4Q174, 4Q246	Texts 174 and 246 from Qumran Cave 4
11QPs^a	The Psalter from Qumran Cave 11, copy a
11QtgJob	The Targum of Job from Qumran Cave 11
CD	Damascus Document from the Cairo Genizah

Places of Publication

EC	Englewood Cliffs, NJ
GC	Garden City, NY
GR	Grand Rapids, MI
Nash	Nashville, TN
NY	New York, NY
Phl	Philadelphia, PA

PAUL
AND HIS
THEOLOGY

Part One

PAUL

Introduction

3 **(I) Paul's Name.** In his letters the Apostle calls himself *Paulos*, the name also used in 2 Pet 3:15 and from Acts 13:9 on. Prior to that in Acts he is called *Saulos* (7:58; 8:1,2; 9:1, etc.), the Gk form of *Saoul*. The latter spelling is found only in the Conversion Accounts (Acts 9:4,17; 22:7,13; 26:14) and stands for the Hebr *Šā'ûl*, the name of the first king of ancient Israel (e.g., 1 Sam 9:2,17; cf. Acts 13:21). It means "asked" (of God *or* of Yahweh). Acts 13:9 marks the transition from "Saul" to "Paul" (except for the later *Saoul*): *Saulos de, ho kai Paulos*, "Saul, also known as Paul." The name *Paulos* is the Gk form of the well-known Roman *cognomen*, "family name," *Paul(l)us*, used by the Aemilian gens, the Vettenii, and the Sergii. One can only conjecture how Paul got such a Roman name. It is pure coincidence that Saul begins to be called Paul in the account in Acts where the Roman proconsul Sergius Paulus is converted (13:7–12); for it is hardly likely that Paul assumed the name of this illustrious Roman convert from Cyprus (*pace* Jerome, *In Ep. ad. Philem.* 1: PL 26.640; H. Dessau and others). More likely, the Apostle was called *Paulos* from birth, and *Saoul* was the *signum* or *supernomen*, "added name," used in Jewish circles. Many Jews of the period had two names, one Semitic (Saul) and the other Greek or Roman (Paul); cf. Acts 1:23; 10:18; 13:1. The names were often chosen for their similarity of sound. There is no evidence that "Saul" was changed to "Paul" at the time of his conversion; indeed, *Saulos* is used in Acts even after this event. The change in 13:9 is probably due to different sources of Luke's information. *Paulus* in Latin means "small, little," but it had nothing to do with Paul's stature or modesty.

(Dessau, H., "Der Name des Apostels Paulus," *Hermes* 45 [1910] 347–68. Harrer, G. H., "Saul Who Also Is Called Paul," *HTR* 33 [1940] 19–33. Lambertz, M., "Zur Ausbreitung des Supernomen oder Signum im römischen Reiche," *Glotta* 4 [1913] 78–143.)

4   (II) Sources and Chronology of Paul's Life. What little is known about Paul comes to us from two main sources: (1) passages in his genuine letters, principally 1 Thess 2:1–2,17–18; 3:1–3a; Gal 1:13–23; 2:1–14; 4:13; Phil 3:5–6; 4:15–16; 1 Cor 5:9; 7:7–8; 16:1–9; 2 Cor 2:1,9–13; 11:7–9,23–27,32–33; 12:2–4,14,21; 13:1,10; Rom 11:1c; 15:19b,22–32; 16:1; and (2) Acts 7:58; 8:1–3; 9:1–30; 11:25–30; 12:25; 13:1–28:31. (Details in the Deutero-Pauline and Pastoral Epistles are of dubious value and can only be used to support what is known from the other two sources.)

5   The two sources mentioned, however, are not of equal value. In the reconstruction of Paul's life, preference must be given to what Paul has told us about himself, for Luke's story of Paul's missionary activity is colored by his pronounced literary tendencies and theological concerns. Recent writers such as J. Knox, D. W. Riddle, R. Jewett, G. Lüdemann, J. Murphy-O'Connor have tried to work out a "life" of Paul or a chronology of his letters either solely or mainly on the basis of his own writings, often expressing a reluctance to admit information from Acts. Yet, puzzling enough, such writers admit details that Luke alone recounts—details that they *need* for their varying solutions (e.g., the appearance of Paul before Gallio [18:12], Paul's 18-month sojourn in Corinth [18:11], or the Lystran origin of Timothy [16:2]). In the following reconstruction of Paul's career I shall use caution and a critical sense and admit details for which Acts is the sole source, provided that they do not contradict or conflict with Pauline data. (The reader will note that my account uses the past tense for Pauline data, but the present tense for data from Acts.)

6   Years ago T. H. Campbell ("Paul's 'Missionary Journeys' ") showed that in the Pauline passages mentioned above there is a sequence of Paul's movements from his conversion to the arrival in Rome that parallels the more detailed movements in Acts. In the accompanying chart I adapt his fundamental study, making use of more recent discussions of the data and adding references to Paul's collaborators.

Letters	Acts
Conversion near Damascus (implied in Gal 1:17c)	Damascus (9:1–22)
To Arabia (Gal 1:17b)	
Return to Damascus (1:17c): 3 yrs	

Letters	Acts
Flight from Damascus (2 Cor 11:32–33)	Flight from Damascus (9:23–25)
To Jerusalem (Gal 1:18–20)	To Jerusalem (9:26–29)
"The regions of Syria and Cilicia" (Gal 1:21–22)	Caesarea and Tarsus (9:30)
	Antioch (11:26a)
	(Jerusalem [11:29–30; 12:25]; –→ 25 below)
	Mission I: Antioch (13:1–4a)
	Seleucia, Salamis, Cyprus (13:4b–12)
Churches evangelized before Macedonian Philippi (Phil 4:15)	South Galatia (13:13–14:25)
	Antioch (14:26–28)
"Once again during 14 years I went up to Jerusalem" (for "Council," Gal 2:1)	Jerusalem (15:1–12)
Antioch Incident (Gal 2:11–14)	Antioch (15:35); Mission II
	Syria and Cilicia (15:41)
	South Galatia (16:1–5)
Galatia (1 Cor 16:1) evangelized for the first time (Gal 4:13)	Phrygia and North Galatia (16:6)
	Mysia and Troas (16:7–10)
Philippi (1 Thess 2:2 [= Macedonia, 2 Cor 11:9])	Philippi (16:11–40)
Thessalonica (1 Thess 2:2; cf. 3:6; Phil 4:15–16)	Amphipolis, Apollonia, Thessalonica (17:1–9)
	Beroea (17:10–14)
Athens (1 Thess 3:1; cf. 2:17–18)	Athens (17:15–34)
Corinth evangelized (cf. 2 Cor 1:19; 11:7–9)	Corinth for 18 months (18:1–18a)
Timothy arrives in Corinth (1 Thess 3:6), probably accompanied by Silvanus (1 Thess 1:1)	Silas and Timothy come from Macedonia (18:5)
	Paul leaves from Cenchreae (18:18b)
	Leaves Priscilla and Aquila at Ephesus (18:19–21)
Apollos (in Ephesus) urged by Paul to go to Corinth (1 Cor 16:12)	Apollos dispatched to Achaia by Priscilla and Aquila (18:17)
	Paul to Caesarea Maritima (18 22a)
	Paul to Jerusalem (18:22b)
	In Antioch for a certain amount of time (18:22c)
Northern Galatia, second visit (Gal 4:13)	Mission III: North Galatia and Phrygia (18:23)

Letters	**Acts**
Ephesus (1 Cor 16:1–8)	Ephesus for 3 yrs or 2 yrs, 3 mos (19:1–20:1; cf. 20:31)
Visit of Chloe, Stephanas, and others to Paul in Ephesus (1 Cor 1:11; 16:17), bringing letter (7:1)	
Paul imprisoned (? cf. 1 Cor 15:32; 2 Cor 1:8)	
Timothy sent to Corinth (1 Cor 4:17; 16:10)	
Paul's second "painful" visit to Corinth (2 Cor 13:2); return to Ephesus	
Titus sent to Corinth with letter "written in tears" (2 Cor 2:13)	
(Paul's plans to visit Macedonia, Corinth, and Jerusalem/Judea, 1 Cor 16:3–8; cf. 2 Cor 1:15–16)	(Paul's plans to visit Macedonia, Achaia, Jerusalem, Rome, 19:21)
Ministry in Troas (2 Cor 2:12)	
To Macedonia (2 Cor 2:13; 7:5; 9:2b–4); arrival of Titus (2 Cor 7:6)	Macedonia (20:1b)
Titus sent on ahead to Corinth (2 Cor 7:16–17), with part of 2 Cor	
Illyricum (Rom 15:19)?	
Achaia (Rom 15:26; 16:1); Paul's third visit to Corinth (2 Cor 13:1)	3 mos in Greece (Achaia) (20:2–3)
	Paul starts to return to Syria (20:3), but goes via Macedonia and Philippi (20:3b–6a)
	Troas (20:6b–12)
	Miletus (20:15c–38)
	Tyre, Ptolemais, Caesarea (21:7–14)
(Plans to visit Jerusalem, Rome, Spain [Rom 15:22–27])	Jerusalem (21:15–23:30)
	Caesarea (23:31–26:32)
	Journey to Rome (27:1–28:14)
	Rome (28:15–31)

7   Differences in the foregoing outline of Paul's movements are to be noted: (1) Luke's failure to mention Paul's withdrawal to "Arabia" (Gal 1:17b); (2) Luke's grouping of Paul's missionary activities in three blocks (I: 13:1–14:28; II: 15:36–18:22; III: 18:23–21:16). Some critics think that Mission I is a completely Lucan fabrication; but no little part of the problem is the question of sources in this part of Acts. (3) Luke's occasion for Paul's escape from Damascus: a plot made by Jews (Acts 9:23; contrast 2 Cor 11:32).

(4) Luke's depiction of Paul "consenting" to the death of Stephen (Acts 7:58–8:1; cf. 22:20), whereas Paul himself speaks only of persecuting "the church of God" (Gal 1:13) or "the church" (Phil 3:6) and never mentions Stephen.

8   The foregoing outline yields at best only a relative chronology. In Paul's own letters the only incident that can be dated extrabiblically is his Damascus escape (2 Cor 11:32–33): The ethnarch of King Aretas closed off the city to take Paul captive, but he escaped by being let down in a basket through a window in the city wall (cf. Acts 9:24–25). That occurred at the end of Paul's three years in Damascus (Gal 1:17c–18). Because Damascus was apparently under Roman rule until Tiberius' death (March 16, AD 37; cf. Josephus, *Ant.* 18.5.3 § 124) and the Nabatean Aretas IV Philopatris (9 BC–AD 39) was given control over it by the emperor Gaius Caligula, Paul's escape must have occurred between AD 37 and 39, probably in AD 39 (see PW 2/1 [1895] 674). Paul's conversion was about three years earlier, probably in AD 36.

9   As for Acts, extrabiblical data are found for five events in Paul's career. In *descending* order of importance, these are:

(1) The proconsulate of L. Junius Gallio Annaeus in Achaia, before whom Paul is haled in Corinth (Acts 18:12). This is the "one link between the Apostle's career and general history that is accepted by all scholars" (J. Murphy-O'Connor, *St. Paul's Corinth*, 141), even though it is reported solely by Luke. Gallio's proconsulship is mentioned in a Gk inscription set up in a temple of Apollo and discovered by E. Bourguet at Delphi in 1905 and 1910. It is fragmentary, and the full publication of all the fragments (by A. Plassart) took place only in 1970. It is a copy of a letter sent by Claudius to the city of Delphi about its depopulation problems.

> [1] Tiber[ius Claudius Caes]ar Au[gus]tus Ge[rmanicus, invested with tribunician po]wer [2] [for the 12th time, acclaimed Imperator for t]he 26th time, F[ather of the Fa]ther[land . . . sends greetings to . . .]. [3] For a l[ong time I have been not onl]y [well disposed toward t]he ci[ty] of Delph[i, but also solicitous for its [4] pro]sperity, and I have always guar[ded th]e cul[t of t]he [Pythian] Apol[lo. But] [5] now [since] it is said to be desti[tu]te of [citi]zens, as [L. Jun]ius [6] Gallio, my fri[end] an[d procon]sul, [recently reported to me, and being desirous that Delphi] [7] should continue to retain [inta]ct its for[mer rank, I] ord[er you (pl.) to in]vite [well born people also from [8] ot]her cities [to Delphi as new inhabitants and to] [9] all[ow] them [and their children to have all the] privi[leges of Del]phi [10] as being citi[zens on equal and like (basis)]. For i[f] so[me . . .] [11] were to trans[fer as citi]zens [to these regions. . . .]

(The rest is inconsequential; my translation follows J. H. Oliver's text, and brackets enclose restorations.)

From this text we may deduce that Gallio was proconsul in Achaia in the 12th year of the reign of Claudius, after the latter's 26th acclamation as "imperator." Whereas the tribunician power, with which the emperor was invested each year, marked his regnal years, acclamation as imperator was sporadic, being accorded to him after triumphs or important military victories. To date an event by it, one must know when the specific acclamation occurred. From other inscriptions one knows that the 22d to 25th acclamations took place in Claudius' 11th regnal year and that the 27th occurred in his 12th year, before August 1, AD 52 (*CIL* 6.1256; Frontinus, *De Aquis* 1.13). The 26th acclamation could have occurred before winter in AD 51 or in the spring of AD 52. But the 12th regnal year began on January 25, AD 52, and a Carian inscription combines the 26th acclamation with the 12th regnal year (*dēmarchikēs exousias to dōdekaton . . . autokratora to eikoston kai hekaton*, BCH 11 [1887] 306–7; A. Brassac, *RB* 10 [1913] 44; cf. *CIL* 8, 14727).

Achaia was a senatorial province, governed by a proconsul appointed by the Roman senate. Such a provincial governor was normally in office for a year and was expected to take his post by June 1 (Dio Cassius, *Rom. Hist.* 57.14.5) and to leave for it by mid-April (ibid., 60.11.6; 60.17.3). Claudius' letter mentions that Gallio had reported to him about conditions in Delphi. Hence, Gallio was already in Achaia and had reported in the late spring or early summer of AD 52. This could have been toward the end of Gallio's proconsular year (June AD 51 to May AD 52) or at the beginning of such a year (June AD 52 to May AD 53). Because Seneca, Gallio's younger brother, says that Gallio developed a fever in Achaia and "took ship at once" (*Ep.* 104.1), it seems that Gallio cut short his stay in Achaia and hurried home. That suggests that Gallio had been there in the late spring and summer of AD 52 and left it not later than the end of October (before *mare clausum*, when sea travel became impossible). Hence, Paul would have been haled before Gallio in the summer or early fall of AD 52. Having been in Corinth for 18 months, Paul would have arrived there in early AD 51 (see Acts 18:11).

(Bourget, E., *De rebus delphicis imperatoriae aetatis capita duo* [Montpellier, 1905]. Brassac, A., "Une inscription de Delphes et la chronologie de saint Paul," *RB* 10 [1913] 36–53, 207–17. Murphy-O'Connor, J., *St. Paul's Corinth* [1983] 141–52, 173–76. Oliver, J. H., "The Epistle of Claudius Which Mentions the Proconsul Junius Gallio," *Hesperia* 40 [1970] 239–40. Plassart, A., "L'Inscription de Delphes mentionnant le proconsul Gallion," *REG* 80 [1967] 372–78; *Les inscriptions du temple du IV siècle* [Fouilles de Delphes III/4; Paris, 1970] § 286.)

10   (2) The expulsion of Jews from Rome by the emperor Claudius (Acts 18:2c), related by Luke to the arrival of Aquila and Priscilla in Corinth, with whom Paul eventually stays. Suetonius (*Claudii vita* 25) reports: Iudaeos impulsore Chresto assidue tumultuantes Roma expulit, "He expelled from Rome Jews who were making constant disturbances at the instigation of

Chrestus." If "at the instigation of *Chrestos*" (which in Suetonius' day would have been pronounced as *Christos*) is a garbled way of referring to disputes over whether Jesus was Christ, Suetonius would be reporting strife at Rome between Jews and Jewish Christians. A fifth-century Christian historian, P. Orosius (*Hist. adv. pag.* 7.6.15–16; CSEL 5.451), quotes Suetonius' text and dates the expulsion in the 9th regnal year of Claudius (January 25, AD 49 to January 24, AD 50). But because Orosius says that Josephus tells of this expulsion, whereas the Jewish historian says nothing of it, his testimony has appeared suspect to some scholars. No one knows where Orosius got his information about the 9th year. This date of the expulsion, however, remains the most likely (see E. M. Smallwood, *The Jews under Roman Rule* [SJLA 20; Leiden, 1976] 211–16; R. Jewett, *Chronology* [1979] 36–38; G. Howard, *ResQ* 24 [1981] 175–77). But some scholars have tried rather to interpret Suetonius' testimony as a reference to a decision made by Claudius in his first regnal year (AD 41) reported by Dio Cassius (*Rom. Hist.* 60.6.6). The emperor, noting the increasing number of Roman Jews, "did not drive them out," but rather ordered them "not to hold meetings" (see G. Lüdemann, *Paul*, 165–71; J. Murphy-O'Connor, *St. Paul's Corinth*, 130–40). This, however, is unconvincing, since Dio Cassius says explicitly that Claudius did *not* expel the Jews (at that time). He may well have expelled *some* Jews later on, as Suetonius affirms. (Dio Cassius' history for AD 49 exists only in epitomes.) However, one must prescind from the Lucan hyperbole, "all the Jews" (Acts 18:2), and ask how "recently" Aquila and Priscilla would have come from "Italy" (not specifically Rome). If the Claudian expulsion was an event in the 9th regnal year, Paul's arrival in Corinth would have been sometime after that.

11 (3) The famine in the reign of Claudius (Acts 11:28b) is not easily dated. It apparently affected the whole eastern Mediterranean area for several years; some evidence suggests that it occurred in Judea about the beginning of the procuratorship of T. Julius Alexander (AD 46 to AD 48; cf. Josephus, *Ant.* 20.5.2 § 101). On its relation to the so-called Famine Visit, → 25, 27 below.

12 (4) Porcius Festus succeeded Felix as procurator of Judea (Acts 24:27). The precise date of this succession is difficult to establish, but it may have occurred *ca.* AD 60 (see E. Schürer, *HJPAJC* 1, 465–66; J. Finegan, *HBC*, 322–24). On the arrival of Festus, Paul appeals to Caesar for a trial (Acts 25:9–12).

13 (5) The recall of Pontius Pilate to Rome in AD 36 to answer for his conduct (see Josephus, *Ant.* 18.4.2 § 89). The removal of Pilate and the arrival of the new prefect Marcellus may be a plausible occasion for the lynching of Stephen (Acts 8:1). Paul's conversion may be related to these events.

Paul's Career

14 **(I) Youth and Conversion. (A) Paul's Youth.** The date of Paul's birth is unknown. He called himself an "old man" (*presbytēs*) in Phlm 9, that is, someone between 50 to 56 years of age (*TDNT* 6, 683); this would mean he was born in the first decade AD. Luke depicts Saul as a "youth" (*neanias*) standing at the stoning of Stephen, that is, as between 24 and 40 years old (cf. Diogenes Laertius 8.10; Philo, *De cher.*, 114).

15 Paul has not told us where he was born, but his name *Paulos* would connect him with some Roman town. He boasted of his Jewish background and traced his lineage to the tribe of Benjamin (Rom 11:1; Phil 3:5; 2 Cor 11:22). He was an "Israelite" (ibid.), "a Hebrew, born of Hebrews . . . , as to the law a Pharisee" (Phil 3:6), one "extremely zealous for the traditions of my fathers' and one who excelled his peers "in Judaism" (Gal 1:14). In calling himself a "Hebrew" (*Hebraios*), he may have meant that he was a Greek-speaking Jew who could also speak Aramaic (see C. F. D. Moule, *ExpTim* 70 [1958–59] 100–102) and could read the OT in the original. Paul's letters, however, reveal that he knew Greek well and could write it and that in addressing Gentile churches he usually quoted the OT in Greek. Traces of Stoic rhetorical diatribe in his letters (→ Pauline Theology, 12) show that he had a Gk education.

16 Luke also presents Paul as "a Jew," as "a Pharisee" born in Tarsus, a Hellenistic town of Cilicia (Acts 22:3,6; 21:39), as having a sister (23:16), and as a Roman citizen from birth (22:25–29; 16:37; 23:27). If Luke's information about Paul's origins is correct, it helps explain both the Hellenistic and Jewish background of Paul.

Tarsus is first attested as *Tarzi* on the ninth-century BC Black Obelisk of Shalmaneser III (1.138; cf. D. D. Luckenbill, *ARAB* 1, 207). In the fourth century Xenophon (*Anab.* 1.2.23) called it "a great and prosperous city," and Gk coins from the fifth and fourth centuries reveal its early Hellenization. It was heavily hellenized by Antiochus IV Epiphanes (175–164 BC), who also established a colony of Jews there (*ca.* 171 BC) to foster commerce and industry. See W. M. Ramsay, *ExpTim* 16 (1904–5) 18–21; cf. Philostratus, *Vita Apoll.* 6.34; A. N. Sherwin-White, *Roman Society*, 144–93.

17 In Pompey's reorganization of Asia Minor in 66 BC, Tarsus became the capital of the province of Cilicia. Later on, freedom, immunity, and citizen-ship were granted to the town by Mark Antony, and Augustus confirmed these rights, which may explain Paul's Roman connections. Tarsus was a well-known center of culture, philosophy, and education. Strabo (*Geogr.*

14.673) knows of its schools as surpassing those of Athens and Alexandria, and of its students as native Cilicians, not foreigners. Athenodorus Cananites, a Stoic philosopher and teacher of the Emperor Augustus, retired there in 15 BC and was given the task of revising the city's democratic and civic processes. Other philosophers, Stoic and Epicurean, also settled and taught there. Famous Romans visited Tarsus: Cicero, Julius Caesar, Augustus, Mark Antony, and Cleopatra. Hence the Lucan Paul can boast that he is a "citizen of no mean town" (Acts 21:39).

> (Böhlig, H., *Die Geisteskultur von Tarsus* [Göttingen, 1913]. Welles, C. B., "Hellenistic Tarsus," *MUSJ* 38 [1942] 41–75. Jones, A. H. M., *The Cities of the Eastern Roman Provinces* [Oxford, 1971] 192–209.)

18   The Lucan Paul also boasts of being "brought up in this city [Jerusalem] and educated at the feet of Gamaliel" (Acts 22:3), that is Gamaliel I, the Elder, whose *floruit* in Jerusalem was *ca.* AD 20 to AD 50 (see W. C. van Unnik, *Tarsus or Jerusalem: The City of Paul's Youth* [London, 1962]). Though the Lucan picture of Paul's youth spent in Jerusalem may explain his Semitic training and mode of thought, Paul himself never utters a word about this feature of his youth. Moreover, it creates a difficulty: Paul's writings never suggest that he encountered or had any personal acquaintance with the Jesus of history (cf. 2 Cor 5:16; 11:4, which need not mean that he had, even though some commentators so understand 5:16)—if he spent his youth in Jerusalem, how could he have escaped such an encounter? Though Paul's mode of argumentation and use of the OT resemble those of contemporary learned Palestinian Jews, his dependence on rabbinical traditions are more alleged than proven (see E. P. Sanders, *Paul and Palestinian Judaism* [Phl, 1977], but cf. J. Neusner, *HR* 18 [1978] 177–91). In the long run the only evidence that Paul was trained by a rabbinical figure such as Gamaliel is the statement in Acts.

19   According to J. Jeremias (*ZNW* 25 [1926] 310–12; 28 [1929] 321–23), at his conversion Paul was not merely a rabbinical disciple (*talmîd hākām*), but a recognized teacher with the right to make legal decisions. This authority would have been presupposed in his going to Damascus to arrest Christians (Acts 9:1–2; 22:4–5; 26:12) and in his voting against Christians as a member of the Sanhedrin (26:10). From this Jeremias concluded that, since 40 was the age required for rabbinical ordination, Paul would have been converted in middle age and have been married, for marriage was also required of rabbis. Jeremias harmonizes the foregoing Lucan data with Pauline material in interpreting 1 Cor 7:8 ("I say to the unmarried and the widowed, 'It is good for them to remain as I am'") to mean that Paul was classing himself with the widowed (*chērai*) rather than with the unmarried (*agamoi*). Again, 1 Cor 9:5 would mean that Paul had not remarried. But almost every point in this intriguing view is dubious: questionable harmonization, Paul's age, the late date for the rabbinical evidence used, Paul's status. See further E. Fascher, *ZNW* 28 (1929) 62–69; G. Stählin, *TDNT* 9, 452 n. 109.

20 (B) Paul's Conversion. Paul wrote of the crucial turn in his life in Gal 1:16: "God was pleased to reveal his son to/in me so that I might preach him among the Gentiles." This revelation followed upon a career in Judaism and a persecution of "the church of God" (1:13; cf. Phil 3:6 and A. J. Hultgren, *JBL* 95 [1976] 97–111). After it he withdrew to "Arabia" (1:17b) and then returned to Damascus (1:17c). That the conversion took place near Damascus is inferred from the vb. "returned." Three years later he escaped from Damascus (*ca.* AD 39; → 8 above) and went up to Jerusalem (1:18). Thus, *ca.* AD 36, Paul the former Pharisee became a Christian and an "apostle to the Gentiles" (Rom 11:13). (Depending on how long one reckons Aretas' control over Damascus, the dates of Paul's conversion and flight are differently estimated: G. Lüdemann dates the conversion in AD 30 or 33, the flight in AD 33 or 36; R. Jewett dates the conversion in AD 34, the flight in AD 37.)

21 Paul clearly regarded the experience near Damascus as the turning point in his life and in that sense a "conversion." It was for him an encounter with the risen Lord (*Kyrios*) that he never forgot. When his apostolate was subsequently challenged, he was wont to expostulate, "Am I not an apostle? Have I not seen Jesus our Lord?" (1 Cor 9:1; cf. 15:8). As a result of that "revelation of Jesus Christ" (Gal 1:12), he became "a servant of Christ" (Gal 1:10), someone with a compulsion (*ananke*, 1 Cor 9:16) to preach the gospel of Christ, and for it he became "all things to all human beings" (1 Cor 9:22).

22 Paul's conversion should not be regarded as the result of the human condition described in Rom 7:7–8:2, as if that were an autobiographical account of his experience. Paul as a Christian looked back on his Jewish career with a robust conscience: "as for righteousness under the law, I was blameless" (Phil 3:6b). He was not crushed by the law. The psychological origins of Paul's experience remain largely inaccessible to us, but in any case there was a "reversal or transvaluation of values" (J. G. Gager) that led to a new understanding of himself as an apostle of the gospel among the Gentiles and to an interpretation of the Christ-event under different images (for more on the meaning of Paul's conversion, → Pauline Theology, 13–15).

23 Luke also associates Paul's conversion with a persecution of the church—in Jerusalem, because of which (Hellenist Jewish) Christians scattered to Judea and Samaria (Acts 8:1–3) and farther (9:2; 11:19). Luke recounts the Damascus experience three times in Acts: once in a narrative that depicts Paul ending with a sojourn for several days in Damascus (9:3–19—but with no mention of a withdrawal to Arabia); and twice in speeches, before a crowd in Jerusalem (22:6–16) and before Festus and King Agrippa (26:12–18). Each of these accounts stresses the overwhelming and unexpected character of the experience that occurred during Paul's persecution of Christians. Puzzling, however, are the variant details in the accounts: whether Paul's companions stand by speechless or fall to the ground; whether or not they hear the heavenly voice; though Jesus addresses Paul "in the 'Hebrew' language," he quotes a Gk proverb (26:14). The failure to harmonize such details reflects Luke's lack of concern for consistency. Yet in each account the essential message is conveyed to Paul: "Saul, Saul, why do you persecute me?"—"Who are you, Sir?"—"I am Jesus (of Nazareth) whom you are persecuting."

(On the "conversion": Bornkamm, G., "The Revelation of Christ to Paul on the Damascus Road and Paul's Doctrine of Justification and Reconciliation," *Reconciliation and Hope* [Fest. L. L. Morris; ed. R. J. Banks; GR, 1974] 90–103. Dupont, J., "The Conversion of Paul, and Its Influence on His Understanding of Salvation by Faith," *Apostolic History and the Gospel* [Fest. F. F. Bruce; eds. W. W. Gasque and R. P. Martin; GR, 1970] 176–94. Gager, J. G., "Some Notes on Paul's Conversion," *NTS* 27 [1980–81] 697–704. Menoud, P.-H., "Revelation and Tradition," *Int* 7 [1953] 131–41. Stanley, D. M., "Paul's Conversion in Acts: Why Three Accounts?" *CBQ* 15 [1953] 315–38. Wood, H. G., "The Conversion of St. Paul: Its Nature, Antecedents and Consequences," *NTS* 1 [1954–55] 276–82. Meinardus, O. F. A., "The Site of Paul's Conversion at Kaukab," *BA* 44 [1981] 57–59.)

24 (II) Paul's Visits to Jerusalem. According to Paul's letters he visited Jerusalem twice after his conversion, once after three years (Gal 1:18) and "once again during fourteen years" (Gal 2:1). In Rom 15:25 he planned another visit, before going to Rome and Spain.

25 According to Acts, however, Paul visits Jerusalem after his conversion five or possibly six times: (1) 9:26–29, after his flight from Damascus; cf. 22:17; (2) 11:29–30, Barnabas and Saul bring a collection from Antioch to the brethren of Judea—related by Luke to the famine in the days of Claudius (→11 above); (3) 12:25, Barnabas and Saul go up to Jerusalem (again? some mss. read rather "from" [Jerusalem], which would mean their return to Antioch after the foregoing visit; but *eis*, "to," is the preferred reading); (4) 15:1–2, the visit of Paul and Barnabas at the "Council"; (5) 18:22, after Mission II, Paul goes up and greets the church before going down to Antioch; (6) 21:15–17, the visit at the end of Mission III, when Paul is arrested.

The correlation of the Pauline and Lucan data about the visits to Jerusalem after the conversion is the most difficult aspect of any reconstruction of Paul's life. The best solution is to equate the Lucan visit 1 with Gal 1:18 and to regard Lucan visits 2, 3, and 4 as references to the same event, the "Council" (= Gal 2:1–10). Luke has undoubtedly historicized and made separate visits out of references to one visit found in different sources. The Lucan visit 5 creates no problem, and visit 6 is that planned by Paul in Rom 15:25.

26 Thus, after Paul escaped from Damascus in AD 39, he came to Jerusalem for the first time *historēsai Kēphan* (Gal 1:18), the meaning of which is debated: "to get information from Cephas" or "to visit Cephas." During his 15 days there he met James, "the Lord's brother," but none of the other apostles; he was otherwise personally unknown to the churches of Judea. According to the Lucan version of this visit 1, Barnabas introduces Paul to the "apostles" and tells them how he has preached boldly in Damascus in the name of Jesus. Paul circulates in Jerusalem among them, continuing to preach boldly and provoking the Hellenists who seek to kill him (Acts 9:27–29).

27 After the 15 days in Jerusalem, according to Gal 1:21 Paul retired to Syria and Cilicia; for how long he does not say. About this time he must have had the vision to which he refers in 2 Cor 12:2–4; it occurred 14 years before 2 Cor was written but is scarcely to be equated with the conversion experience. According to Acts 22:17–21 Paul has an ecstasy while praying in the Jerusalem Temple during visit 1. It is the danger presented by the provoked Hellenists that leads the brethren to bring Paul from Jerusalem to Caesarea and to send him off to Tarsus (Acts 9:30). Acts does not specify how long Paul stays in this city of Cilicia, but the sequence makes a number of years not improbable (perhaps AD 40 to AD 44). The stay ends with a visit from Barnabas, who brings him back to Antioch, where he remains a whole year (11:25–26), engaged in evangelization. Luke relates visit 2 to Jerusalem, the "Famine Visit," to this period.

(Meeks, W. A., and R. Wilken, *Jews and Christians in Antioch* [Missoula, MT, 1978].)

28 **(III) Pauline Missions.** Acts organizes Paul's missionary activity into three segments, but "If you had stopped Paul on the streets of Ephesus and said to him, 'Paul, which of your missionary journeys are you on now?' he would have looked at you blankly without the remotest idea of what was in your mind" (J. Knox, *Chapters*, 41–42). Yet the trouble is not solely Lucan; it stems from the way we read Acts, since Luke does not distinguish Mission I, II, or III, as moderns tend to count them. Yet we have seen (→ 6 above) that there is a certain correlation in the Pauline and Lucan data for Paul's missionary journeys, apart from the first. His journeys cover roughly AD 46 to AD 58, the most active years of his life, as he evangelized Asia Minor and Greece.

29   (A) Mission I (AD 46 to AD 49). The story of this pre-"Council" mission is recounted solely by Acts (13:3–14:28) and is confined to essentials to suit Luke's literary purpose (cf. 2 Tim 3:11). Paul has given us no details about his missionary activity in the pre-"Council" period of 14 years (Gal 2:1). For a time he was in "the areas of Syria and Cilicia" and was "preaching the faith" (Gal 1:21,23) "among the Gentiles" (Gal 2:2). When he later wrote Phil, he recalled that "at the beginning of the evangelization, no church except you shared with me in the matter of giving and receiving, when I left Macedonia" (Phil 4:15). As he left Macedonia then (*ca.* AD 50; → 39 below), there were other churches, presumably evangelized by Paul. But where were they? Since he passed to Philippi in Macedonia from Asia Minor, he could be referring to churches of S Galatia in the account of Mission I (Acts 13:13–14:25) —or less likely to those of N Galatia, Mysia, or Troas at the beginning of Mission II (→ 38 below). In any case, Macedonia was scarcely the first area evangelized by Paul (*pace* M. J. Suggs, *NovT* 4 [1960] 60–68), and the account of Mission I in Acts does not contradict the sparse Pauline details.

30   Moved by the Spirit, Antiochene prophets and teachers impose hands on Barnabas and Saul and send them forth in the company of John Mark, Barnabas' cousin (Col 4:10). They depart from Seleucia, the port of Syrian Antioch, head for Cyprus, and pass through the island from Salamis to Paphos. There the proconsul Sergius Paulus is converted (Acts 13:7–12). From Paphos the missionaries sail for Perga in Pamphylia (on the S coast of central Asia Minor), where John Mark deserts Barnabas and Paul and returns to Jerusalem. Barnabas and Paul make their way to towns in S Galatia: to Pisidian Antioch, Iconium, Lystra, and Derbe. In Antioch, Paul preaches first to Jews in their synagogue; and when he meets resistance, Paul announces his turning henceforth to the Gentiles (13:46). After evangelizing the area and meeting opposition from Jews in various town (even stoning in Iconium), Paul and Barnabas retrace their steps from Derbe through Lystra, Iconium, and Pisidian Antioch to Perga and sail from Attalia for Syrian Antioch, where Paul spends "no little time" with Christians (14:28). One of the issues that surfaces in Mission I is the relation of the new faith to Judaism, and more specifically the relation of Gentile Christians to older Jewish converts. Are the Gentile converts to be circumcised and required to observe the Mosaic Law? (See G. Ogg, *Chronology*, 58–71.)

31   (B) "Council" Visit (AD 49). According to Luke, during Paul's stay in Antioch (end of Mission I) converts from Judea arrive and begin to insist on circumcision as necessary for salvation (15:1–3). When this leads to a dispute between them and Paul and Barnabas, the Antiochene church sends Paul, Barnabas, and others up to Jerusalem to consult the apostles and elders about the status of Gentile converts. This visit results in the so-called Council of Jerusalem.

32 In Gal 2:1–10 Paul told of this visit; he went up to Jerusalem with Barnabas and Titus "once again during 14 years" (to be reckoned from his conversion, i.e., in the year 49–50). Paul spoke of this visit as the result of "a revelation" (2:2), and he laid before "those of repute" in Jerusalem the gospel that he had been preaching to the Gentiles, and they "added nothing" to it. James, Cephas, and John realized the grace given to Paul and Barnabas and extended to them the right hand of fellowship—uninfluenced by the "false brethren" who had slipped in to spy out the freedom (from the law) gained in Christ and to whom Paul had not yielded "so that the truth of the gospel might be preserved" (2:4–5). The issue settled on this occasion was circumcision: it was not obligatory for salvation, and Titus, though a Greek, was not forced to be circumcised.

33 The first part of Acts 15 (vv 4–12) deals with this same doctrinal issue. Those whom Paul labelled "false brethren" are here identified as "some believers from the sect of the Pharisees" (15:5). When the matter is debated by the apostles and elders, Peter's voice seemingly prevails, and the assembly acquiesces in his decision (based on his own experience in Acts 10:1–11:18). The Jerusalem "Council" thus frees the nascent church from its Jewish roots and opens it to the world apostolate then confronting it. Paul's position is vindicated.

34 **(C) Antioch Incident (AD 49).** After the Jerusalem "Council," Paul went down to Antioch, and before long Peter followed. At first both of them ate with Gentile Christians, but soon "some people from James" (Gal 2:12), i.e., Christians with pronounced Jewish leanings, arrived and criticized Peter for eating with Gentile converts. Yielding to their criticism, Peter separated himself, and his action led other Jewish Christians, even Barnabas himself, to do the same. Paul protested and opposed Peter to his face, because he was "not walking according to the truth of the gospel" (2:11). It may be implied that Paul was successful in his criticism, but even so the disciplinary question of Jewish dietary regulations for Gentile converts was posed anew. (Cf. R. E. Brown and J. P. Meier, *Antioch and Rome*, 28–44.)

35 **(D) Jerusalem Decree on Dietary Matters.** Paul's opposition to Peter did not solve the dietary problem at Antioch. Emissaries seem to have been sent again to Jerusalem, presumably after Paul's and Peter's departure from Antioch. James convenes the apostles and elders again, and their decision is sent as a letter to the local churches of Antioch, Syria, and Cilicia (Acts 15:13–19). Paul himself has said nothing about this decision, and even in Acts he is only subsequently informed about it by James on his arrival in Jerusalem after Mission III (21:25).

36 Acts 15 is a problematic and composite chapter, in which Luke has undoubtedly telescoped two incidents that were distinct in subject and time. To be noted: (1) Verses 1–2 are a literary suture joining information from different sources. (2) Verse 34 is missing in the best Gk mss., but added in the Western textual tradition to explain where Silas was at the beginning of Mission II. (If v 34 is omitted, Silas' location becomes a problem: When does he join Paul on Mission II?) (3) Simeon (15:14), who is usually identified as Simon Peter (and has to be so understood in Luke's telescoped story), was probably someone else in the source used. For elsewhere in Acts, Peter is called *Petros* (15:7) or *Simōn Petros* (10:5; 18:32), but never *Symeōn*. In Luke's source the Simeon of 15:14 may well have been Simeon Niger, one of the prophets or teachers of Antioch (13:1); he is probably sent as one of the emissaries to James of Jerusalem about the dietary regulations. (4) Peter's speech about circumcision and the Mosaic law (15:7–11) scarcely coincides with the topic discussed by James (15:14–21).

37 As a result of the consultation, James sends a letter to Antioch, Syria, and Cilicia (15:22–29), recommending that Gentile Christians in such mixed communities abstain from meat sacrificed to idols, from blood, from the meat of strangled animals, and from illicit sexual unions. It would have been sent with Judas Barsabbas and Silas (15:22) to Antioch and to Paul and Barnabas, presumed to be still there. Acts 15:35–36 mentions Paul and Barnabas preaching in Antioch; but this should be understood of their sojourn immediately following the "Council," after which Paul would have left Antioch for Mission II. Paul learns about the letter later (21:25).

> (On relating Acts 15 to Gal 2 and the problem of Paul's visits to Jerusalem: Benoit, P., "La deuxième visite du Saint Paul à Jérusalem," *Bib* 40 [1959] 778–92. Dupont, J., "Pierre et Paul à Antioche et à Jérusalem," *RSR* 45 [1957] 42–60. Funk, R. W., "The Enigma of the Famine Visit," *JBL* 75 [1956] 130–36. Giet, S., "Le second voyage de Saint Paul à Jérusalem," *RevScRel* 25 [1951] 265–69; "L'Assemblée apostolique et le décret de Jérusalem: Qui était Simeon?" *RSR* 39 [1951] 203–20; "Les trois premiers voyages de Saint Paul à Jérusalem," *RSR* 41 [1953] 321–47; "Nouvelles remarques sur les voyages de Saint Paul à Jérusalem," *RevScRel* 31 [1957] 329–42. Parker, P., "Once More, Acts and Galatians," *JBL* 86 [1967] 175–82. Rigaux, B., *Letters*, 68–99. Strecker, G., "Die sogenannte zweite Jerusalemreise des Paulus (Acts 11,27–30)," *ZNW* 53 [1962] 62–77.)

38 **(E) Mission II (AD 50 to AD 52).** According to Acts 15:37–39, Paul refuses to take John Mark with him on Mission II because of his earlier defection. Instead, Silas accompanies Paul, and setting out from Antioch they make their way through Syria and Cilicia to the towns of S Galatia, Derbe, and Lystra (where Paul takes Timothy as a companion, having had him circumcised, Acts 16:1–3!). From there he passes through Phrygia to N Galatia (Pessinus, Ancyra, and Tavium) and founds new churches. Hindered from moving to Bithynia, he goes on from Galatia into Mysia and Troas. Here he seems to have been joined by Luke—or at least data from Luke's diary begin at this point (Acts 16:10–17, the first of the "We-Sections").

39   In response to a dream-vision Paul passes over to Neapolis, the port of Philippi, and the latter becomes the site of his first Christian church in Europe (→ 6 above). After imprisonment and flogging at Philippi because he has exorcised a slave girl who had been the source of much gain for her master, he passed on to Thessalonica via Amphipolis and Apollonia (2 Thess 2:1; Acts 17:1–9). His short stay in Thessalonica is occupied by evangelization and controversy with Jews; it ends with his flight to Beroea (17:10), and eventually to Athens (17:15). Here Paul tries to interest Athenians, renowned for their love of novel ideas, in the gospel of the risen Christ (17:22–31). But he fails: "We'll listen to you on this topic some other time" (17:32). After this disappointment, Paul moves on to Corinth (AD 51), at that time one of the most important towns in the Mediterranean world. (For a collection of ancient descriptive texts about Corinth and a report of archaeological work, see J. Murphy-O'Connor, *St. Paul's Corinth.*) Here Paul lives with Aquila and Priscilla (18:2–3), Jewish Christians recently come from Italy (→10 above) and tentmakers by trade like Paul (see R. F. Hock, *JBL* 97 [1978] 555–64). During his stay in Corinth, which lasts for 18 months, he converts many Jews and Greeks and founds a vigorous predominantly Gentile Christian church. In AD 51 Paul wrote his first letter to the THESSALONIANS. Near the end of his stay (AD 52; → 9 above), Paul is haled before the proconsul L. Junius Gallio, who dismisses the case as a matter of words, names, and Jewish law (18:15). Some time later Paul withdraws from Corinth, sailing from its port of Cenchreae for Ephesus and Caesarea Maritima. After paying a visit to the Jerusalem church (18:22), he goes to Antioch, where he stays well over a year (possibly from late autumn of AD 52 until the spring of AD 54).

(Davies, P. E., "The Macedonian Scene of Paul's Journeys," *BA* 26 [1963] 91–106. Ogg, G., *Chronology*, 112–26.)

40   (F) **Mission III (AD 54 to AD 58).** Leaving Antioch (Acts 18:23), Paul travels overland once again through N Galatia and Phrygia to Ephesus. The capital of the province of Asia becomes the center of his missionary activity for the next three years (Acts 20:31), and for "two years" he lectures in the hall of Tyrannus (19:10). Shortly after his arrival in Ephesus Paul wrote GALATIANS (*ca.* AD 54). To this missionary period also belong the letter to the PHILIPPIANS and possibly that to PHILEMON (ca. AD 56–57). Acts says nothing of an imprisonment of Paul at Ephesus, but see 1 Cor 15:32; 2 Cor 1:8–9; cf. Phil 1:20–26. Some of the problems that Paul experienced and has described in 2 Cor 11:24–27 may well have happened to him during this period of Ephesian missionary activity.

41   During this time, reports came to Paul about the situation of the Corinthian church. To cope with the situation there—doubts, factions, resentment toward Paul himself, scandals—he wrote at least five letters to Corinth, of which only two survive (one of which is a composite). One letter preceded 1 Cor (see 1 Cor 5:9), warning the Corinthians about associating with immoral Christians (and probably also recommending a collection for the poor of Jerusalem, a question about which the Corinthians sent a subsequent inquiry [see 1 Cor 16:1]). Then, to comment on reports and to answer questions sent to him, Paul wrote 1 CORINTHIANS shortly before Pentecost (probably in AD 57). This letter, however, was not well received, and his relations with the faction-torn church of Corinth worsened. The situation called forth a hasty visit to Corinth (2 Cor 12:14; 13:1–2; 2:1 ["a painful visit"]; 12:21), which really accomplished nothing. On his return to Ephesus, Paul wrote to the Corinthians a third time, a letter composed "with many tears" (2 Cor 2:3–4,9; 7:8,12; 10:1,9). This letter may have been taken by Titus, who visited the Corinthians personally in an attempt to smooth out relations.

42   Probably during Titus' absence the revolt of the Ephesian silversmiths occurs (Acts 19:23–20:1). Paul's preaching of the new Christian "Way" incites Demetrius, a maker of miniature shrines of Artemis of Ephesus, to lead a riotous mob into the theater in protest against Paul and the spread of Christianity.

43   This experience prompted Paul to leave Ephesus and to journey to Troas (2 Cor 2:12) to work. Not finding Titus there, he decided to go on to Macedonia (2:13). Somewhere in Macedonia (possibly at Philippi) he met Titus and learned from him that a reconciliation between Paul and the Corinthians had been worked out. From Macedonia, Paul wrote to Corinth his fourth letter (the Letter A of 2 CORINTHIANS) in the autumn of AD 57. It is not possible to say whether Paul proceeded immediately to Corinth or went first from Macedonia into Illyricum (cf. Rom 15:19), whence he may have written 2 Cor 10–13 (Letter B). Eventually, Paul did arrive in Corinth on his third visit there, probably in the winter of AD 57 and stayed for three months in Achaia (Acts 20:2–3; cf. 1 Cor 16:5–6; 2 Cor 1:16).

44   By this time Paul had been thinking of returning to Jerusalem. Mindful of the injunction of the "Council" that the poor should be remembered (Gal 2:10), he saw to it that his Gentile churches took up a collection for the poor of Jerusalem. This was done in the churches of Galatia, Macedonia, and Achaia (1 Cor 16:1; Rom 15:25–26). Paul planned to take the collection to Jerusalem and thus terminate his evangelization of the eastern Mediterranean world. He wanted to visit Rome (Rom 15:22–24) and from there go on to Spain and the West. During the three-month stay in Achaia, Paul wrote the letter to the ROMANS (probably from Corinth, or its port, Cenchreae [Rom 16:1]) at the beginning of AD 58. (See further R. E. Brown and J. P. Meier, *Antioch and Rome*, 105–27.)

45 When spring arrives, Paul decides to sail from Corinth (Acts 20:3) for Syria. But as he is about to embark, a plot against him is hatched by some Jews; thus, he resolves to travel overland, by way of Macedonia. Disciples from Beroea, Thessalonica, Derbe, and Ephesus accompany him. They spend Passover of AD 58 in Philippi (where Luke rejoins him—Acts 20:5, a "We-Section"). After the feast they leave by ship for Troas and journey overland to Assos, where they take ship again for Mitylene. Skirting the coast of Asia Minor, Paul sails from Chios to Samos, then to Miletus, where he addresses the elders of Ephesus summoned there (Acts 20:17–35). He is not deterred by their prediction of his coming imprisonment, but sails on to Cos, Rhodes, Patara in Lycia, Tyre in Phoenicia, Ptolemais, and Caesarea Maritima. An overland journey brings him to Jerusalem, which he has hoped to reach by Pentecost of AD 58 (20:16; 21:17). (See G. Ogg, *Chronology*, 133–45.)

46 **(IV) Paul's Last Imprisonment.** For the rest of Paul's career we are dependent solely on the Lucan information in Acts; it covers several years after AD 58, during which he endures a long captivity.

47 **(A) Last Visit to Jerusalem and Arrest (AD 58).** Arriving in Jerusalem, Paul and his companions pay their respects to James in the presence of the elders of that church (Acts 21:18). James immediately realizes that Paul's presence in Jerusalem may cause a disturbance among Jewish Christians. So he counsels Paul to join four men who are about to go through the Nazirite vow ceremony and to pay the expenses for them as a gesture of good will toward Jewish Christians. Paul consents, and the seven-day ceremonial period is almost over when he is seen in the Temple precincts by Jews from the province of Asia. They accuse him of advocating violation of the Mosaic law and of defiling the sanctity of the Temple by bringing a Greek into it. They set upon him, drag him from the Temple, and try to kill him. He is saved, however, by the tribune of the Roman cohort stationed in the Fortress Antonia. The tribune eventually puts Paul under protective arrest (22:27) and brings him before the Sanhedrin. But fear of the Jews makes the tribune send Paul to the procurator of Judea, Antonius Felix, residing in Caesarea Maritima (23:23–33). Felix, who expects Paul to bribe him (24:26), keeps Paul in prison for two years (AD 58 to AD 60).

48 **(B) Appeal to Caesar; Journey to Rome (AD 60).** When the new procurator Porcius Festus arrives (possibly *ca.* AD 60; →12 above), Paul "appeals to Caesar," i.e., requests a trial in Rome (25:11), by virtue of his Roman citizenship. Festus has to grant this request. (See A. N. Sherwin-White, *Roman Society*, 48–70.)

Escorted by a Roman centurion (and probably by Luke, as the "We-Sections" indicate), he sets sail from Caesarea Maritima for Sidon and passes Cyprus to come to Myra in Lycia. In the late autumn of AD 60 (27:9) they leave Myra on an Alexandrian ship bound for Italy, expecting bad weather. Their route takes them first to Cnidus (on the S coast of Asia Minor), then southward "under the lee of Crete off Salmone" as far as Fair Havens, near the Cretan town of Lasea (27:7–8). When they try to reach the harbor of Phoenix, a northeaster blows up and carries them for days across the Adriatic to Malta, where they are finally shipwrecked (28:1).

49   After spending the winter on Malta, Paul and his escort sail for Syracuse in Sicily, then for Rhegium (modern Reggio di Calabria), and lastly for Puteoli (modern Pozzuoli, near Naples). Their overland journey to Rome takes them through Appii Forum and Tres Tabernae (28:15). Paul arrives in the capital of the empire in the spring of AD 61 and for two years is kept under house arrest (AD 61 to AD 63) with a soldier to guard him. This situation, however, does not deter him from summoning Roman Jews to his quarters and evangelizing them (28:17–28). Traditional interpretation ascribes Paul's writing of PHILEMON, COLOSSIANS, and EPHESIANS to this imprisonment. (See A. N. Sherwin-White, *Roman Society*, 108–19; R. E. Brown, *The Churches*, 47–60.)

50   **(C) End of Paul's Life.** Acts ends with the brief account of Paul's house arrest. His arrival in Rome and his unhindered preaching of the gospel there form the climax of the story of the spread of the word of God from Jerusalem to the capital of the civilized world of the time—Rome—which symbolizes "the end of the earth" (Acts 1:8). But this was not the end of Paul's life. The mention of "two whole years" (28:30) does not imply that he died immediately thereafter, no matter what interpretation is given to the enigmatic ending of Acts.

51   The PASTORAL LETTERS (Titus; 1 and 2 Tim) have often been regarded as genuine writings of Paul and have been considered as composed by him after his Roman house arrest. Indeed, they suggest that he visited the East again (Ephesus, Macedonia, and Greece). According to them Paul would have set up Titus as the head of the Cretan church and Timothy as the head of the Ephesian church. 2 Tim purports to be Paul's last will and testament, written as he was about to face death. It suggests that he may have been arrested at Troas (4:13) and brought to Rome again (1:17), where this letter would have been written from prison. But these letters are usually regarded today as pseudepigraphical, possibly written by a disciple of Paul (cf. R. E. Brown, *The Churches*, 31–46).

52 For other details about the end of Paul's life we are dependent on later ecclesiastical traditions, which became heavily laced with legend. Did Paul ever visit Spain? Perhaps little more than a historicization of plans expressed in Rom 15:24,28 is involved; subsequent tradition tells us of Paul, freed after two years of house arrest, going to Spain. Clement of Rome (*I Cor.* 5.7) records that Paul "taught the whole world uprightness and traveled to the extreme west (*epi to terma tēs dyseōs elthōn*). And after he had borne witness before the authorities, he was taken from this world and went to the holy place, having proved himself the greatest model of endurance." Clement's testimony (*ca.* AD 95) suggests the visit to Spain, another trial, and martyrdom. *Ca.* AD 180 the Muratorian fragment (lines 38–39; *EB* 4) implies that the last part of Acts, recounting "the departure of Paul from the City [Rome] as he set out for Spain," has been lost.

53 Eusebius (*HE* 2.22.3) is the first to mention Paul's second imprisonment in Rome and his martyrdom under Nero: "After defending himself, [Paul] was again sent on the ministry of preaching, and coming a second time to the same city suffered martyrdom under Nero. During this imprisonment he wrote the second epistle to Timothy, indicating at the same time that his first defense had taken place and that his martyrdom was at hand." Eusebius further quotes Dionysius of Corinth (*ca.* AD 170), who stated that Peter and Paul "were martyred at the same time" (*HE* 2.25.8). Tertullian (*De praescr.* 36) compares Paul's death with that of John (the Baptist), i.e., by beheading.

The Eusebian testimony about Paul's death in the persecution of Nero is widely accepted. This persecution lasted, however, from the summer of AD 64 to the emperor's death (June 9, AD 68); and it is hard to pinpoint the year of Paul's martyrdom. The notice of Dionysius of Corinth that Peter and Paul "were martyred at the same time" (*kata ton auton kairon*) has often been understood to mean in the same year, but the preferred year for the death of Paul is AD 67, toward the end of Nero's persecution, as Eusebius' account seems to suggest. This chronology, however, is not universally accepted and is not without its difficulties.

54 Paul is said to have been buried on the Via Ostiensis, near the site of the modern basilica of San Paolo fuori le Mura. In AD 258, when Christian tombs in Rome were threatened with desecration during the persecution of Valerian, Paul's remains were transferred for a time to a place called *Ad Catacumbas* on the Appian Way. Later they were returned to their original resting place, over which Constantine built his basilica.

(Meinardus, O. F. A., "Paul's Missionary Journey to Spain: Tradition and Folklore," *BA* 41 [1978] 61–63. Pherigo, L. P., "Paul's Life after the Close of Acts," *JBL* 70 [1951] 277–84.)

Part Two

PAULINE THEOLOGY

Introduction

3 (I) Aims, Limits, and Problems. A sketch of Pauline theology must take into account the character of the Apostle's writings, which do not offer a systematic presentation of his thought. Most of what Paul wrote was composed ad hoc—to handle concrete problems by letters. In them he developed certain topics and exhorted his churches to the practice of a more intense Christian life. Almost every extant letter exemplifies this twofold purpose. This also explains how he could mingle elements of revelation, fragments of the primitive kerygma, teachings of Christ, interpretations of the OT, a personal understanding of the Christ-event, and even his own private opinions. Any attempt, therefore, to sketch Pauline "theology" must try to reckon with the varied nuances of the Apostle's thought and expression.

Moreover, a presentation of "Pauline" theology is an admission that Paul's view of the Christian experience is but one among several theologies in the NT. It is imperative to respect Paul's theology and not confuse it with John's, Luke's, or any other's. It must be studied in and for itself. This caution is not meant to imply that a NT theology is impossible or that contradictions are to be expected between Paul and other NT writers. The NT as a whole bears witness to a faith in one Lord, one baptism, one God and Father of all (Eph 4:5–6), and a theology explaining that one faith is not an impossibility. But such a presentation will be the richer if nuances of individual NT writers are respected.

4 A sketch of Pauline theology is a systematization of the Apostle's thought in a form in which he himself did not present it. If such a systematization forces his thought into categories foreign to it or attempts merely to line up "proofs" for a theological system born of another inspiration, it has little value. The effort to synthesize Paul's thought must respect his categories as far as possible, with due allowance for the unequal degree of his affirmations and the diversity of the formative contexts. The guiding principle of such a sketch, therefore, cannot be an extrinsic one, be it Aristotelian, Thomistic, Hegelian, or Heideggerian.

5 Though the primary aim is a descriptive presentation of Paul's view of Christian faith, this sketch also intends to be a normative theological presentation. It aims above all at determining what Paul meant when he wrote to the Christians whom he immediately addressed, but it also aims at ascertaining what his theology means for Christians of today. This sketch is not merely a study of Paul's thought as a historian of religion (agnostic or believer) might present it; it does not attempt merely to determine what Paul taught, what influenced him, or how his teachings fit into the general history of Hellenistic, Jewish, or Christian ideas. Paul's theology is an exposition of the inspired biblical heritage of early Christians, and the Word of God proposed in his exposé still has an existential meaning for the faith of people today. In this way, Paul's theology is a *part* of normative biblical theology, just as biblical theology itself is only a part of normative theology as such. There are two poles in biblical theology, one descriptive, the other normative.

6 The "meaning for the faith of people today" cannot be something completely other than the meaning intended by Paul for his contemporaries. Any attempt to understand him that fails to recognize a radical homogeneity between his meaning "now" and "then" fails to bring *his* inspired message to people today. A valid sketch of Pauline theology must, therefore, ascertain first of all what Paul meant, and in this sense it must be descriptive. The means to achieve this are not the logic or metaphysics of some philosophical system foreign to him, however legitimate or fruitful such a transposition might be for other purposes. The means are rather those of philological, historical, and literary criticism, joined to an empathy of Christian faith. In other words, the one who sketches Paul's theology in a descriptive presentation shares with Paul the same faith and seeks through it to determine his meaning for today. Although biblical theologians, in trying to discover what Paul meant, employ the same tools of interpretation used by historians of religion—or, for that matter, by interpreters of any ancient document—they also affirm that through Paul "the one Lord . . . the one God and Father of us all" is communicating an inspired message to them and the people of their time. The fundamental presupposition is the inspired character of the Pauline corpus, a matter of *faith*. Paul's exposé and understanding of Christian faith are sketched in a way that is meaningful and relevant for Christians of a later age.

7   This empathy of Christian faith is sometimes expressed in terms of the "analogy of faith," a phrase derived ultimately from Paul himself (Rom 12:6). It may not be used to insist that the totality of Christian faith has to be found in Paul or even that his thought *must* be interpreted according to the sense of later dogmatic progress, with its precisions and specific nuances. If a seminal notion formulated by Paul has in time undergone further dogmatic development because of a polemical situation or a conciliar decision in the church, then that seminal notion must be recognized as such. It may be that the seminal notion is expressed by Paul in a vague, "open" fashion; and thus formulated, it could conceivably (by philological criteria) have developed in one way or another. But the further dogmatic development may have removed that *openness* of formulation, so far as Christian tradition is concerned. Yet this does not mean that the historian of dogma or the dogmatic theologian can insist that this later development is the precise meaning of a text of Paul. Such scholars have no charism whereby they can read more in an "open" Pauline text than can the exegete or biblical theologian. To understand the "analogy of faith" in such a way as to read back into Paul a later meaning would be false to him and to the inspired autonomy of his conception and formulation. Rather, that analogy must be understood in terms of the total Pauline biblical faith. Obviously, the biblical theologian is not content merely with the interpretation of individual passages in their immediate context (that is, with exegesis). One seeks to express the total Pauline message, which transcends the contextual situation and embraces also the relational meaning of Pauline utterances.

Though normative biblical theology is only a part of the larger complex of Christian theology, it does enjoy its own autonomy of formulation and conception. While only inceptive, for it cannot be regarded as the full answer to theological problems of today, it is privileged: It attempts to formulate synthetically what the witnesses of the early Christian tradition were inspired to set down in their own way. It deals immediately and exclusively with a form of Christian tradition that alone enjoys the distinctive divine charism of inspiration. True, for a Christian the continued guidance of the Spirit has guarded the authentic dogmatic developments of later times from contradicting the seminal formulations and conceptions. But such protection does not mean that the full flower is already present in the seed. Hence the need to respect Pauline theology for what it is.

(Barr, J., "Biblical Theology," *IDBSup* 104–11. Käsemann, E., "The Problem of a New Testament Theology," *NTS* 19 [1972–73] 235–45. Merk, O., "Biblische Theologie: II. Neues Testament," *TRE* 6, 455–77. Richardson, A., 'Historical Theology and Biblical Theology," *CJT* 1 [1955] 157–67. Stendahl, K., "Biblical Theology, Contemporary," *IDB* 1, 418–32. Strecker, G. [ed.], *Das Problem der Theologie des Neuen Testaments* [WF 367; Darmstadt, 1975].)

8   This sketch of Pauline theology reckons with seven uncontested letters of the Pauline corpus: 1 Thess, Gal, Phil, 1 and 2 Cor, Rom, and Phlm. Today three letters of that corpus, 2 Thess, Col, and Eph, are disputed and often considered to be Deutero-Pauline (i.e., written by a disciple of Paul). The three "Pastoral Letters" (Titus, 1 and 2 Tim) create a still greater problem; their relation to the two foregoing groups of letters is at best pseudepigraphical. Following the lead of other modern Catholic interpreters, we shall omit the data from the Pastorals. References to the Deutero-Paulines, when called for, will be set in parentheses. The theology of Heb is a problem apart and is not treated as Pauline. Material in Acts related to Paul's teaching can at best be used for comparative purposes, for it really forms part of the Lucan portrait of Paul and is more properly part of Lucan theology.

9   Can one detect any development in Paul's teaching? This is a debated issue. Those who in the past admitted a development were often reckoning with a corpus of ten or more Pauline letters; and so, for instance, it was not difficult to detect a development in Paul's ecclesiological teaching, as one moved from the uncontested letters to Col and Eph, and then on to the Pastorals. But that alleged development is precisely part of the reason why one distinguishes the Pauline Letters as in § 8 above. The majority view today queries whether a development can be detected in the seven letters that constitute the uncontested group (see W. G. Kümmel, *NTS* 18 [1971–72] 457–58). Yet one can note at times differences in issues (often of minor importance) that reveal some development. For instance, in the early letter, 1 Thess 4:14, one finds only an extrinsic connection between Christ's resurrection and the glorious resurrection of Christians: Through Jesus, God will lead with him those who have died. It is thus set forth in an apocalyptic description of the *eschaton*, reflecting the primitive eschatology of the early church. Later on one notes a more intimate connection between the passion, death, and resurrection of Christ and human beings who find salvation in him. Christ has become a "power," producing new life in Christian believers, which eventually ensures their resurrection and life "with Christ" (see Phil 3:10–11; cf. Rom 6:4). Again, Paul's treatment of the role of the Mosaic law in human life develops from Gal to Rom (→ 95 below).

(Allo, E.-B., "L'Evolution' de l'évangile de Paul," *VP* 1 [1941] 48–77, 165–93. Buck, C. and G. Taylor, *Saint Paul: A Study of the Development of His Thought* [NY, 1969]. Dodd, C. H., "The Mind of Paul, I and II," *New Testament Studies* [Manchester, U.K., 1953] 67–128. Hurd, J. C., *The Origin of I Corinthians* [London, 1965] 8–12. Lester-Garland, L. V., "The Sequence of Thought in the Pauline Epistles," *Theology* 33 [1936] 228–38. Lowe, J., "An Examination of Attempts to Detect Development in St. Paul's Theology," *JTS* 42 [1941] 129–42.)

10   **(II) Paul's Background.** Five factors that influenced Paul's theology may be considered; not all of them are of equal importance.

(A) Pharisaic, Jewish Background. The polemical passages in which Paul reacts against the Mosaic law should not be allowed to obscure the fact that even the Christian Paul looked back with pride on his life as a Jew of the Pharisaic tradition (Phil 3:5–6; Gal 1:14; 2 Cor 11:22). This strong Jewish background accounts for the fact that he thinks and expresses himself in OT categories and images. It also accounts for his abundant use of the OT, which he cites explicitly almost 90 times (yet never in 1 Thess, Phil, or Phlm). Though his use of the OT is often similar to that of the authors of Qumran and other intertestamental Jewish literature, he usually quotes it according to the LXX. At times, he accommodates the OT text or gives new meaning to passages he cites (e.g., Hab 2:4 in Rom 1:17 or Gal 3:11; Gen 12:7 in Gal 3:16; Exod 34:34 in 2 Cor 3:17); he may allegorize a text (Gen 16:15; 17:16 in Gal 4:21–25) or wrest it from its original context (Deut 25:5 in 1 Cor 9:9). Paul's use of the OT does not conform to our modern ideas of quoting Scripture, but it does conform to the contemporary Jewish way of interpreting it and must be judged in that light. That he was inspired by the Spirit to interpret it in this fashion does not mean that his interpretation always reveals a hidden, deeper (literal) sense otherwise unsuspected. Yet his Jewish background makes him quote the OT to stress the unity of God's action in both dispensations and often as announcing the Christian gospel (Rom 1:2) or preparing for Christ (Gal 3:24). Even if he contrasts the "letter [of the law] and the Spirit" (2 Cor 3:6; Rom 2:29; 7:6), the OT is still for him a means through which God speaks to humanity (1 Cor 9:10; 2 Cor 6:16–17; cf. Rom 4:23; 15:4). Indeed, most of his theology (in the narrow sense, teaching about God) and his anthropology (teaching about human beings) clearly reveal this Jewish background.

11   Luke depicts Paul as trained by a rabbi in Jerusalem (→ Paul, 18), but Paul himself never says anything about his "rabbinical" background. Though he has identified himself as a former Pharisee (Phil 3:5), as a member of the Jewish group out of which came the later rabbinic tradition, one must use discernment in appealing to such literature to illustrate his Jewish background, for the vast majority of it was not put in writing until the time of Rabbi Judah the Prince at the beginning of the third century AD.

(Bring, R., "Paul and the Old Testament," *ST* 25 [1971] 21–60. Byrne, B., *'Sons of God'—'Seed of Abraham* [AnBib 83; Rome, 1979]. Davies, W. D., "Paul and the Dead Sea Scrolls: Flesh and Spirit," *The Scrolls and the New Testament* [ed. K. Stendahl; NY, 1957] 157–82. Ellis, E. E., *Paul's Use of the Old Testament* [GR, 1981]. Espy, J. M., "Paul's 'Robust Conscience' Re-examined," *NTS* 31 [1985] 161–88. Fitzmyer, J. A., "The Use of Explicit Old Testament Quotations in Qumran Literature and in the New Testament," *ESBNT*, 3–58. Murphy-O'Connor, J. [ed.], *Paul and Qumran* [Chicago, 1968]. Sanders, E. P., *Paul and Palestinian Judaism* [Phl, 1977].
    On the rabbinic issue: Daube, D., *The New Testament and Rabbinic Judaism* [London, 1956]. Davies, W. D., *Jewish and Pauline Studies* [Phl, 1984]; *Paul and Rabbinic Judaism* [Phl, 1980].)

12 (B) Hellenistic Background. Despite Paul's heavily Jewish way of thinking, factors such as his use of a Roman name, his appeal to the OT in Greek, and his composition of letters in Greek reveal him to have been a diaspora Jew. Though he does not write literary Koine, his style betrays a good Gk education (→ Paul, 16–18). Attempts to detect Aramaisms in Paul's Greek (see W. C. van Unnik, *Sparsa collecta* [NovTSup 29; Leiden, 1973] 129–43) have not been successful, even though Paul, in calling himself a "Hebrew" (Phil 3:5), may mean that he also spoke Aramaic, a Semitic language widely used in his day in Syria and Asia Minor.

Even if Paul had not been trained as a professional *rhētōr*, his mode of composition and expression often reveals the influence of Gk rhetoric. See H. D. Betz's analysis of Gal according to Greco-Roman rhetoric and epistolography (*Galatians* [Hermeneia; Phl, 1979] 14–25). Traces are found in his letters of the Cynic-Stoic mode of argumentation called *diatribē*, a mode of discourse conducted in familiar, conversational style and developed by lively debate with an imaginary interlocutor; its sentence structure is often short, and questions are interjected; antitheses and parallel phrases often punctuate the development (see J. Nélis, *NRT* 70 [1948] 360–87). Good examples of this style are found in Rom 2:1–20; 3:1–9; 9:19; 1 Cor 9. It was once fashionable to ascribe to Paul's Hellenistic background such terms as "Lord," "Son of God," "flesh and spirit," and "mystery" and to ascribe to Hellenistic gnosticism his use of "Adam" and "Man," a redeemer myth, preexistence, instrumentality in creation, etc. But many of these terms and notions have been shown to have been at home in first-century Judaism, even in Palestine itself, which in the last pre-Christian centuries had come to grips with Hellenistic influence and the use of the OT in Greek.

Whereas Jesus' illustrations often reflect the agrarian life of Galilee, Paul frequently uses images derived from city-culture, especially Hellenistic. He uses Gk political terminology (Phil 1:17; 3:20), alludes to Gk games (Phil 2:16; 1 Cor 9:24–27), employs Gk commercial terms (Phlm 18) or legal terminology (Gal 3:15; 4:1–2; Rom 7:1), and refers to Hellenistic slave trade (1 Cor 7:22; Rom 7:14) or Hellenistic celebrations in honor of a visiting emperor (1 Thess 2:19). He employs the Hellenistic ideas of *eleutheria*, "freedom" (Gal 5:1,13) and *syneidēsis*, "conscience" (1 Cor 8:7,10,12; 10:25–29; 2 Cor 5:11; Rom 2:15), and the Stoic ideas of *autarkeia*, "sufficiency, contentment" (2 Cor 9:8) and *physis*, "nature" (Rom 2:14). Note especially the Hellenistic vocabulary in Phil 4:8: *prosphilēs*, "amiable," *euphēmos*, "well-sounding," *aretē*, "moral excellence," and *epainos*, "something praiseworthy." In 1 Cor 15:33 he even quotes Menander, *Thais*, frg. 218. This Hellenistic influence is detected more in Paul's ethical teaching than in his theology proper.

(Betz, H. D., *Der Apostel Paulus und die sokratische Tradition* [BHT 45; Tübingen, 1972]. Broneer, O., "Paul and the Pagan Cults at Isthmia," *HTR* 64 [1971] 169–87. Bultmann, R., *Der Stil der paulinischen Predigt und die kynisch-stoische Diatribe* [FRLANT 13; Göttingen, 1910]. De Witt, N. W., *St. Paul and Epicurus* [Minneapolis, 1954]. Hugedé, N., *Saint Paul et la culture grecque* [Geneva, 1966]. Koester, H., "Paul and Hellenism," *The Bible in Modern Scholarship* [ed. P. J. Hyatt; NY, 1965] 187–95. Pfitzner, V. C., *Paul and the Agon Motif* [NovTSup 16; Leiden, 1967]. Stowers, S. K., *Diatribe and Paul's Letter to the Romans* [SBLDS 57; Chico, CA, 1981].)

13   (C) The Revelation to Paul. Paul's theology was influenced most of all by his experience near Damascus and by his faith in the risen Christ as the Son of God that developed from that experience. Today NT scholars are less prone than those of former generations to look on that experience merely as a psychological "conversion" to be explained in terms of Paul's Jewish background or of Rom 7, understood as an autobiographical account. Paul himself speaks of that experience as a revelation of the Son accorded him by the Father (Gal 1:16); in it he "saw Jesus the Lord" (1 Cor 9:1; cf. 1 Cor 15:8). That revelation of the crucified "Lord of glory" (1 Cor 2:8) not only turned Paul the Pharisee into an apostle but also made him the first Christian theologian. The only difference between that experience, in which Christ appeared to him (1 Cor 15:8), and the experience of the official witnesses of the resurrection (1 Cor 15:5–7) was that his vision occurred much later. It put him on an equal footing with the Twelve and others who had seen the Lord. He spoke of it as an event in which he had been "seized" by Christ Jesus (Phil 3:12), and a "necessity" had been laid upon him to preach the gospel to the Gentiles (1 Cor 9:16; cf. Gal 1:16b). He compared that experience to God's creation of light: "For God who said, 'Let light shine out of darkness,' has shone in our hearts to give the light of the knowledge of God's glory on the face of Christ" (2 Cor 4:6). The compulsion of divine grace pressed him into the service of Christ. His response was one of vivid faith, in which he confessed with the early church that "Jesus is Lord" (1 Cor 12:3; cf. Rom 10:9; Phil 2:11). In a creative act, that experience illumined Paul's mind and gave him an insight into what a disciple later called "the mystery of Christ" (Eph 3:4).

14   (1) That "revelation" (Gal 1:12,16) impressed Paul with the unity of divine action for the salvation of all humanity, which is manifest in both the Old and New Dispensations. As a result of that encounter with the risen Christ, Paul did not become a Marcionite, rejecting the OT. The Father who revealed his Son to Paul was the same God that Paul the Pharisee had always served. He was the creator, the lord of history, the God who continually saved his people Israel, and who proved to be a faithful lord of the covenant despite Israel's infidelities. Probably because he had been a Pharisee preoccupied with the minutiae of the law, Paul never manifested a profound understanding of that "covenant," so infrequently does he speak of it. Yet his experience near Damascus did not alter his fundamental commitment to the "one God."

(2) That vision taught him the soteriological value of the death and resurrection of Jesus the Messiah in God's salvific plan. If his basic *theology* did not change, his christology did. As a Jew, Paul had shared the messianic expectations of his people (see Dan 9:25; 1QS 9:11), looking forward to the coming of a messiah (of some sort). But the vision of the risen Christ taught him that God's Anointed One had already come, that he was "Jesus our Lord, who was handed over for our offences and raised up for our justification" (Rom 4:25). Before his experience near Damascus, Paul certainly knew that Jesus of Nazareth had been crucified, "hung on a tree," and hence "cursed" in the sense of Deut 21:23 (see Gal 1:13; 3:13). This was undoubtedly one of the reasons why he as a Pharisee could not accept Jesus as the Messiah. Jesus was "a stumbling block" (1 Cor 1:23), one "cursed" by the very law that Paul so zealously observed (Gal 3:13; cf. 1:14). But that revelation impressed him emphatically with the messianic, soteriological, and vicarious value of the death of Jesus of Nazareth in a way that he never suspected before. With a logic that only a Pharisee could appreciate, Paul saw Christ Jesus taking upon himself the law's curse and transforming it into its opposite, so that he became the means of freeing humanity from malediction. The cross, which had been the stumbling block to Jews, became in his eyes the "power and the wisdom of God" (1 Cor 1:24). Henceforth, he would understand that crucified "Lord of glory" (1 Cor 2:8) as his exalted Messiah.

(3) That revelation impressed Paul with a new vision of salvation history. Before the encounter with the Lord, Paul saw human history divided into three great periods: (1) from Adam to Moses (the period without the law); (2) from Moses to the Messiah (the period of the law); and (3) the messianic age (the period when the law would be perfected or fulfilled). The experience near Damascus taught him that the messianic age had already begun; it thus introduced a new perspective into salvation history. The *eschaton*, "endtime," so avidly awaited before, had already started (1 Cor 10:11), although a definitive stage of it was still to be realized (as was hoped, not too far in the future). The Messiah had come, but not yet in glory. Paul realized that he (with all Christians) found himself in a double situation: one in which he looked back upon the death and resurrection of Jesus as the inauguration of the new age, and another in which he still looked forward to his coming in glory, his Parousia.

15   Far more than his Pharisaic background, therefore, or even his Hellenistic cultural roots, that revelation of Jesus gave Paul an ineffable insight into the "mystery of Christ." It enabled him to fashion his "gospel," to preach the fundamental good news of salvation in a form that was distinctively his own. However, Paul did not immediately understand all the implications of the vision accorded him. It provided only a basic insight that was to color all that he was to learn about Jesus and his mission among human beings, not only from the early church's tradition, but also from his own apostolic experience in preaching "Christ crucified" (1 Cor 1:23).

(Beker, J. C., *Paul the Apostle*, 3–10. Jeremias, J., "The Key to Pauline Theology," *ExpTim* 76 [1964] 27–30. Menoud, P.-H., "Revelation and Tradition: The Influence of Paul's Conversion on His Theology," *Int* 7 [1953] 131–41. Munck, J., *Paul and the Salvation of Mankind* [Richmond, VA, 1959] 11–35. Rigaux, B., *Letters*, 40–67. Stob, H., "The Doctrine of Revelation in Paul," *CTJ* 1 [1966] 182–204.)

16 (D) Paul, Jesus, and Early Tradition. If the main inspiration of Paul's theology was the revelation granted near Damascus, that event was not the only source of his knowledge about Christ and the Christian movement. Paul was not the founder of the movement but joined it after missionary activity had already been begun by those who were apostles before him (Gal 1:17). It is a priori likely, then, that Paul inherited from the pioneer tradition of the church at least some ideas about Christ. At first, this observation might seem to contradict what he himself says in Gal about the origin of his gospel, that he was not taught it and that it came to him rather through a revelation of Jesus Christ (1:11,15–17; 2:6). Yet here especially we must be sensitive to the nuances of Paul's expression: These passages in Gal were written in the heat of controversy. Paul had been under attack, accused of not being a real apostle and of preaching only a watered-down version of the gospel because of his attitude toward the law of Moses and Jewish practices. When he wrote Gal, Paul was at pains, then, to emphasize his divine, direct, and undelegated apostolic commission and the heavenly origin of his gospel.

Yet this emphasis must not be allowed to obscure what is found elsewhere in his letters that clearly indicate a dependence on the apostolic tradition of the early church—on its kerygma, liturgy, hymns, confessional formulas, theological terminology, and parenesis. Fragments of the primitive kerygma are found in Paul's letters: 1 Thess 1:10; Gal 1:3–4; 1 Cor 15:2–7; Rom 1:3–4; 4:25; 8:34; 10:8–9. He has incorporated elements of the liturgy into them: the eucharistic formula (of Antiochene origin? 1 Cor 11:23–25); prayers like "Amen" (1 Thess 3:13[?]; Gal 6:18; cf. 1 Cor 14:16; 2 Cor 1:20), "Maranatha" (1 Cor 16:22), "Abba, Father" (Gal 4:6; Rom 8:15); doxologies (Gal 1:5; Phil 4:20; Rom 11:36; 16:27[?]), and hymns (Phil 2:6–11; [cf. Col 1:15–20; Eph 5:14]). His confessional formulas also echo church usage: "Jesus is Lord" (1 Cor 12:3, Rom 10:9), "Jesus Christ" (1 Cor 3:11), or "the Messiah" (Rom 9:5). He inherited as well a number of theological terms, for example, the titles "Lord," "Son of God"; the word "apostle"; the expressions *baptizō eis*, "church of God," etc. Finally, certain hortatory parts of his letters that employ stereotyped terminology suggest that Paul is incorporating parenetic or catechetical material drawn from common usage (1 Thess 4:1–12; 1 Cor 6:9–10; Gal 5:19–21; [Eph 5:5]).

17 At times Paul explicitly calls attention to the fact that he is "handing on" (*paradidonai*) what he has "received" (*paralambanein*); see 1 Cor 11:2,23;

15:1,3. He thus uses the Greek equivalents of the technical vocabulary of tradition paralleled in the rabbinic schools: *māsar lĕ-*, "pass on to"; *qibbēl min*, "receive from." He also appeals to the customs of the churches (1 Cor 11:16) and recommends fidelity to tradition (1 Thess 2:13; Phil 4:9; 1 Cor 11:2; 15:2; Rom 6:17; [cf. 2 Thess 2:15; 3:6]). O. Cullmann (*RHPR* 30 [1950] 12–13) found it surprising that Paul applied such a discredited notion to the normative doctrinal and moral precepts of the primitive community, when he recalled how Jesus reacted precisely to the *paradosis* of the Jews (Mark 7:3–13; Matt 15:2). Obviously, Paul saw something different here; it was for him not merely "the tradition of human beings" (Mark 7:8). Cf. 1 Thess 2:13.

18   Another aspect of Paul's dependence on early church tradition is seen in his acquaintance with what Jesus did and taught. Paul gives no evidence of having known Jesus personally in his earthly ministry (→ Paul, 18); not even 2 Cor 5:16 need imply that he did. Nor should it be imagined that Paul was granted a cinematic view of that ministry at the time of his Damascus experience. It is remarkable how little his letters betray knowledge of Jesus of Nazareth or even of what is recorded about Jesus in the Gospels. One reason for this is that Paul wrote his letters before the Gospels took the form that we know. Yet an even more important reason is that Paul, not having been an eyewitness, emphasizes the salvific effects of the passion, death, and resurrection of Christ, which for him transcend the data of the historical ministry of Jesus. His interest lies in these climactic events of Jesus' career rather than in the minutiae of Jesus' manner of life, his ministry, his personality, or even his message. He may allude to or quote a saying of Jesus occasionally (1 Thess 4:2,15; 5:2,13,15; 1 Cor 7:10–11 [cf. 25]; 9:14; 11:23–25; 13:2; Rom 12:14,17; 13:7; 14:13,14; 16:19), and such allusions or quotations reveal that sayings of Jesus were already being handed on in the early church in addition to the kerygma. But these sayings are invariably referred to by Paul as utterances of "the Lord" (*Kyrios*), a title that immediately reveals the transcendent aspect under which Paul regarded them. He was not interested in Jesus as a teacher, a prophet, or as the chronological source of such transmission. Rather, he was interested in the exalted, risen Lord, who became the real agent of the tradition developing in the bosom of the apostolic church. That is why he attributed to the *Kyrios* what in reality he had derived from the early community. The *Kyrios* is at work in that transmission, and as such he is regarded as "the end of the law" and a replacement of the *paradosis* of the Jews.

19   Paul alludes to remarkably few events of the life of Jesus: He was born of a woman under the law (Gal 4:4), instituted the eucharist (1 Cor 11:23), was betrayed (1 Cor 11:23), was crucified (Gal 2:20; 3:1; Phil 2:8; 1 Cor 2:2,8), died (1 Cor 15:3), was buried (1 Cor 15:4), was raised from the dead (1 Cor

15:5), and taken up to heaven (Rom 10:6 [cf. Eph 4:9]). Yet even these events are not narrated for their own sake or in the manner of the evangelists; they are, instead, recorded in contexts of a peculiarly theological or kerygmatic character. Paul may have learned the outline of Jesus' last days from the early church, but probably some of the details were already known to him before his conversion and were related to his persecution of "the church of God" (Gal 1:13).

20 Such features as these suggest that Paul had derived information from the traditions of early churches (Jerusalem, Damascus, Antioch). Moreover, his visit to Jerusalem, when he spent 15 days with Cephas (Gal 1:18), would support this. But such information was always transformed by Paul's personal vision and insight.

> (Baird, W., "What Is the Kerygma?" *JBL* 76 [1957] 181–91. Bruce, F. F., "Paul and the Historical Jesus," *BJRL* 56 [1973–74] 317–35. Cullmann, O., " 'Kyrios' as Designation for the Oral Tradition Concerning Jesus," *SJT* 3 [1950] 180–97. Dungan, D. L., *The Sayings of Jesus in the Churches of Paul* [Phl, 1971]. Gerhardsson, B., *Memory and Manuscript* [ASNU 22; Lund, 1961] 262–323; *Tradition and Transmission in Early Christianity* [ConNT 20; Lund, 1964]. Hunter, A. M., *Paul and His Predecessors* [Phl, 1981]. Kuss, O., *Paulus*, 440–51. Ridderbos, H. N., *Paul and Jesus: Origin and General Character of Paul's Preaching of Christ* [Phl, 1958]. Stanley, D. M., " 'Become Imitators of Me': The Pauline Conception of Apostolic Tradition," *Bib* 40 [1959] 859–77; "Pauline Allusions to the Sayings of Jesus," *CBQ* 23 [1961] 26–39.)

21   (E) Paul's Apostolic Experience. Another factor in the development of Paul's theology was his experience as an apostle and missionary proclaiming the gospel and founding churches throughout Asia Minor and Europe. How much did his practical experience and concrete contacts with Jews and Gentiles mold his view of Christianity? Would Paul have written as he did on justification or on the relation of the gospel to the law, if it were not for the Judaizing problem that he encountered? The real meaning of the universal scope of Christian salvation probably dawned on Paul as he worked continually with Jews who failed to accept his message and with Gentiles who did heed him. From his earliest letters he reveals an awareness of the privileged position of his fellow Jews in the divine plan of salvation (1 Thess 2:13–14; cf. Rom 1:16; 2:9–10). He wrestled in Rom 9–11 with the problem of the role of Israel in the Father's new plan of salvation by grace and through faith in Christ Jesus. But he was keenly aware that he had been called to preach to the Gentiles (Gal 1:15–16); he calls himself the "apostle of the Gentiles" (Rom 11:13). He admits that he is "indebted to Greeks and to Barbarians" (Rom 1:14). Moreover, the church as the "body" of Christ (1 Cor 12:27–28) is almost certainly the result of his understanding of the Christian *ekklēsia* in the light of the contemporary Greco-Roman understanding of the state as the body politic (→122 below). (The tendency manifested here is carried further by the disciples of Paul who in Col and Eph unite the themes of church, body, and head in a view of the risen Christ as the lord of the *kosmos* and employ the notion of *plērōma*, "fullness.") The problems that Paul himself encountered in founding and governing individual churches were almost certainly responsible for his gradual awareness of what the "church" meant in a transcendent, universal sense. To his apostolic experience must also be attributed a number of references to the Hellenistic world, which are met in various developments of his teaching (see 1 Cor 8:5; 10:20–21; 12:2; Gal 4:9–10).

22 Was part of Paul's apostolic experience a contact with gnostics? This is a highly debated question today. That Paul speaks of *gnōsis*, "knowledge," in a special sense and pits over against his "story of the cross" (1 Cor 1:18) a worldly knowledge is clear. But that he is coping with some form of gnosticism that was invading his communities is another question. Here no little part of the problem is what is meant by "gnosticism." That full-blown gnosticism was already current in the time of Paul is very difficult to admit. There may be elements in Pauline teaching that eventually fed into its full-blown form in the second century AD, but they are at most proto-gnostic elements in his letters. Despite all the claims about gnosticism as a pre-Christian phenomenon, no real evidence of a *pre-Christian* redeemer figure or of such a myth of the primal man has been adduced.

(Cook, R. B., "Paul . . . Preacher or Evangelist?" *BT* 32 [1981] 441–44. Holtz, T., "Zum Selbstverständnis des Apostels Paulus," *TLZ* 91 [1966] 321–30. Kertelge, K., "Das Apostelamt des Paulus, sein Ursprung und seine Bedeutung," *BZ* 14 [1970] 161–81. Lüdemann, G., *Paulus, der Heidenapostel: Band II, Antipaulinismus im frühen Christentum* [FRLANT 130; Göttingen, 1983]. Seidensticker, P., *Paulus der verfolgte Apostel Jesu Christi* [SBS 8; Stuttgart, 1965].

Chadwick, H., "Gnosticism," *OCD*, 470–71. Dupont, J., *Gnosis: La connaissance religieuse dans les épîtres de S. Paul* [Louvain, 1960]. Pagels, E. H., *The Gnostic Paul: Gnostic Exegesis of the Pauline Letters* [Phl, 1975]. Ridderbos, H. N., *Paul*, 27–29, 33–35. Schmithals, W., *Gnosticism in Corinth* [Nash, 1071]; *Paul & the Gnostics* [Nash, 1972]. Yamauchi, E. M., *Pre-Christian Gnosticism: A Survey of the Proposed Evidences* [GR, 1973].)

23 Whatever Paul inherited from his Jewish background, from his contacts with Hellenism, and whatever he later derived from the tradition of the early church and his own missionary activity were all uniquely transformed by his insight into the mystery of Christ accorded to him near Damascus. Other NT writers could claim a Jewish background and Hellenistic contacts, but none of them has Paul's profundity in understanding the Christ-event, except possibly John.

Dominant Perspectives

24   (I) Paul's Christocentric Soteriology. (A) The Key to Pauline Theology. There has been a constant effort to formulate the key to Pauline theology, its essence, its core, or its center. Ever since the Reformation, Lutherans and Calvinists, with varying nuances, have found it in justification by faith—a view still held by many today (e.g., E. Käsemann, W. G. Kümmel). In the nineteenth century, F. C. Baur, using Hegelian philosophy, sought to explain the core in terms of the antithesis between "flesh" (human) and "Spirit" (divine). Subsequently, Liberal Protestant interpreters introduced a more rational, ethical view of the antithesis, expressing it in terms of the (human) spirit and (sensual) flesh. Eventually, W. Wrede, though he belonged to the same movement, sought to find the essence of Pauline Christianity in Christ and his redemptive work. The History of Religions School, using varied data from the mystery-cults of the eastern Mediterranean world, depicted Paul's "religion" in terms of a mystical communion with the crucified and risen Lord through the cultic acts of baptism and eucharist. These nineteenth-century views were eventually analyzed by A. Schweitzer, for whom Paul's theology was rather to be summed up as an eschatological Christ-mysticism. For him Paul's eschatology differed from the consistent eschatology that Schweitzer claimed was that of Jesus, because with the death and resurrection of Jesus the *eschaton* had actually begun for Paul. Believers then shared mystically in the eschatological mode of being of the risen Christ. Forms of these earlier explanations have persisted well into the twentieth century.

25   In this century, R. Bultmann insisted that NT theology "begins with the *kerygma* of the earliest Church and not before" (*TNT* 1.3), that is, it has little to do with the Jesus of history. He also demythologized that *kērygma* and cast it in terms of Heideggerian philosophy so that faith, the response to the *kērygma*, becomes an existential "decision" by which human beings embark on a new way of life that is fully authentic. As for Paul, his "basic position is not a structure of theoretical thought . . . but it lifts the knowledge inherent in faith itself into the clarity of conscious knowing" (*TNT* 1. 190). Thus, Bultmann has, in effect, returned to a nuanced (existentialist) understanding of the antithesis used by F. C. Baur mentioned above and has reduced Paul's theology to an "anthropology," an interpretation of human existence.

Bultmann's exposé of Pauline theology has two main parts: Man Prior to the Revelation of Faith, and Man under Faith. In the first part (Man Prior to Faith) he discusses Paul's anthropological concepts (body, soul, spirit, life, mind and conscience, heart), his treatment of "flesh, sin, and world" (creation, the human condition as *sarx*, "flesh," its relation to the universality of sin, the world, and the law). In the second part (Man under Faith) Bultmann treats the Pauline ideas of God's righteousness, human righteousness as a present reality and gift from God, reconciliation, grace (as an event coming from Christ's salvific death and resurrection), the Word, church, and sacraments; faith (its structure, place in life, and relation to the *eschaton*); freedom (from sin [= walking in the Spirit], law, and death). This justly praised exposé of Paul's teaching is marked by Bultmann's sustained effort to present it in genuinely biblical categories.

26 Such an approach to Paul's teaching is, however, too exclusively a development of Paul's ideas in Rom, to which all else seems to have been made subservient. The reduction of Pauline theology to an anthropology has, in effect, minimized Christ's role (cf. Rom 7:24–8:2), because the salvific events of the first Good Friday and Easter Sunday have been demythologized to the point of being dehistoricized. Again, Christ's role in the life of the individual, called to such an existential decision of faith, has been maximized to the neglect of his role in the corporate and cosmological view of salvation history (cf. Rom 9–11, which Bultmann does not sufficiently consider). This minimizing of the role of Christ stems from a reluctance to admit the "content sense" of Paul's theology, the historical "objective phase" of human redemption, and a concern to recast Pauline teaching in phenomenological terminology. A certain amount of demythologizing of the NT is needed to bring its message to people of the twentieth century, but one still has to reckon with the way Paul himself looked upon the Christ-event in the effort to formulate the key to his theology.

27 More recently, J. C. Beker has coped with the same problem, recognizing both the contingent character of Paul's teaching and its coherent center. The latter he regards as "a symbolic structure in which a primordial experience (Paul's call) is brought into language in a particular way," viz., in "the apocalyptic language of Judaism, in which he [Paul] lived and thought." Thus, he delineated "the Christ-event in its meaning for the apocalyptic consummation of history, that is, in its meaning for the triumph of God" (J. C. Beker, *Paul the Apostle*, 15–16). It would have been better if Beker had written of the "eschatological" consummation of history rather than of its "apocalyptic" consummation. Similarly, "the triumph of God" is too un-Pauline an expression to be the goal of Pauline teaching; it is redolent of E. Käsemann. This has to be said, even when one recognizes the centrality of Christ in Beker's view of the core of Pauline teaching.

28 The key to Pauline theology, however, should be formulated in terms of what the Apostle stated over and over again in various ways: "It pleased God to save those who would believe through the folly of the gospel message [kērygma]. For whereas Jews demand signs and Greeks look for philosophy, we proclaim a Christ who has been crucified, a stumbling block to Jews and an absurdity to Gentiles. But to those who have been called, whether Jews or

Greeks, he is Christ, the power of God and the wisdom of God" (1 Cor
1:21–25; cf. Rom 1:16; 2 Cor 4:4). This "story of the cross" (1 Cor 1:18) thus
puts Christ himself at the center of soteriology (God's new mode of
salvation), and all else in Paul's teaching has to be oriented to this
christocentric soteriology.

29 If Paul's theology is predominantly a christology, one must insist on its
functional character. Paul was little concerned to explain the intrinsic
constitution of Christ *in se*; he preached "Christ crucified," Christ as
significant for humanity: "You are God's children through your union with
Christ Jesus who became for us wisdom from God, our uprightness, our
sanctification, our redemption" (1 Cor 1:30). This "Christ crucified," though
described in figures derived from contemporary Jewish or Hellenistic backgrounds and even embellished with myth, still has relevance for people of the
twentieth century. To understand what Paul meant and still means for people
today one does not merely demythologize his ideas; rather, a certain
remythologization of the twentieth-century mind may be needed. In any case,
what is needed is not a subtractive, but an interpretative demythologization.

(Dahl, N., "Rudolf Bultmann's *Theology of the New Testament*," *The Crucified
Messiah and Other Essays* [Minneapolis, 1974] 90–128, esp. 112–22. Fuller,
R. H., *The New Testament in Current Study* [NY, 1962] 54–63. Käsemann, E.,
NTQT, 13–15.)

30 In our attempt to give a genetic development of Paul's theology, we
shall begin with the term that he himself used to describe his message about
Christ, his "gospel." From such a starting point we can move on to various
aspects of the content of his message.

31 **(B) Paul's Gospel.** *Euangelion* as "the good news of Jesus Christ" is a
specifically Christian meaning of the word, and as such was almost certainly
developed by Paul within the early Christian community (see W. Marxsen,
Mark the Evangelist [Nash, 1969] 117–50). Paul uses the word more
frequently than does any other NT writer: 48 times in his uncontested letters
(it occurs 8 times in the Deutero-Paulines, and 4 times in the Pastorals). In
general, it designates Paul's own personal presentation of the Christ-event.
　Euangelion sometimes denotes the activity of evangelization (Gal 2:7;
Phil 4:3,15; 1 Cor 9:14b,18b; 2 Cor 2:12; 8:18), as does the verb *euangelizesthai*
(used by Paul 19 times; it occurs twice also in the Deutero-Paulines).
Normally, however, *euangelion* denotes the content of his apostolic
message—what he preached, proclaimed, announced, spoke about (see J. A.
Fitzmyer, *TAG*, 160 n. 5). Paul realized that his message had its origin in God
himself: "God's gospel" (1 Thess 2:2,8–9; 2 Cor 11:7; Rom 1:1; 15:16).
Succinctly, its content was for him "the gospel of Christ" (1 Thess 3:2; Gal 1:7;

Phil 1:27) or "the gospel of his Son" (Rom 1:9), wherein the genitive is normally understood as objective, that is, the good news about Christ, even though in some instances one may detect a nuance of Christ as the originator of the gospel (2 Cor 5:20; Rom 15:18–19). More specifically, the gospel is "the good news of the *glory* of Christ" (2 Cor 4:4), i.e., the message about the risen Christ: "We proclaim not ourselves, but Christ Jesus as Lord!" (2 Cor 4:5), giving to Christ the title par excellence for his risen status. Sometimes the content is expressed simply as "the faith" (Gal 1:23), "the word" (1 Thess 1:6), or "the word of God" (2 Cor 2:17).

32 *Euangelion* became Paul's personal way of summing up the meaning of the Christ-event (→ 67 below), the meaning that the person and lordship of Jesus of Nazareth had and still has for human history and existence. Hence, Paul could speak of "my gospel" (Rom 2:16), "the gospel that I preach" (Gal 2:2; cf. 1:8,11), or "our gospel" (1 Thess 1:5; 2 Cor 4:3; cf. 1 Cor 15:1), because he was aware that "Christ did not send me to baptize, but to preach the gospel" (1 Cor 1:7). Though patristic writers (Irenaeus, *Adv. haer.* 3.1,1; Tertullian, *Adv. Marc.* 4.5 [CSEL 47.431]; Origen in Eusebius, *HE* 6.25,6 [GCS 9/2.576]; Eusebius himself, *HE* 3.4,7 [GCS 9/1.194]) sometimes interpreted these Pauline expressions to mean the Lucan Gospel, which they regarded as a digest of Paul's preaching (as the Marcan Gospel was supposed to be of Peter's), nothing so specific as a Gospel-like narrative is meant by these expressions. Paul was fully aware that his commission to preach the good news of God's Son among the Gentiles (Gal 1:16) was not a message wholly peculiar to himself or different from that preached by those "who were apostles before me" (Gal 1:17); "whether it was I or they, so we preach and so you came to believe" (1 Cor 15:11). Paul recognized himself as the "servant" of the gospel (*doulos*, Phil 2:22), conscious of a special grace of apostolate. He thought of himself as set apart like the prophets of old (Jer 1:5; Isa 49:1) from his mother's womb for this task (Gal 1:15; Rom 1:1), being "entrusted" with the gospel as some prized possession (1 Thes 2:4; Gal 2:7). He experienced a "compulsion" (*ananke*, 1 Cor 9:16) to proclaim it and considered his preaching of it as a cultic, priestly act offered to God (Rom 1:9; 15.16). He was never ashamed of the gospel (Rom 1:16); even imprisonment because of it was for him a "grace" (Phil 1:7,16).

33 Various characteristics of the gospel in Paul's sense may be singled out: (1) Its *revelatory* or *apocalyptic* nature. God's salvific activity for his people is now made known in a new way through the lordship of Jesus Christ (Rom 1:17); thus the gospel reveals the reality of the new age, the reality of the *eschaton.* To this apocalyptic nature of the gospel must be related Paul's view of it as *mysterion*, "mystery, secret," hidden in God for long ages and now revealed—a new revelation about God's salvation. In the best mss. of 1 Cor 2:1–2 Paul equates "God's mystery" with "Jesus Christ . . . crucified" (see *app. crit.*), just as he had equated his "gospel" with "Christ crucified" in 1 Cor 1:17,23–24. Paul viewed himself as a "steward," dispensing the wealth of this mystery (1 Cor 4:1). It now reveals to Christians the plan conceived by God and hidden in him from all eternity (1 Cor 2:7) to bring humanity, Gentiles as well as Jews, to share in the salvific inheritance of Israel, now realized in Christ Jesus. Even the partial insensibility of Israel belongs to this mystery (Rom 11:25). In presenting the gospel as "mystery," Paul is implying that it is never fully made known by ordinary means of communication. As something revealed, it is apprehended only in faith; and even when revealed, the opacity of divine wisdom is never completely dispelled. *Mystērion* is an eschatological term derived from Jewish apocalyptic sources; its application to the gospel gives the latter a nuance that *euangelion* alone would not have had, that is, something fully comprehended only in the *eschaton.*

34   In thus coming to speak of the gospel as mystery, Paul is using a word already familiar in contemporary Gk mystery religions. However, the comprehension that he gives to it and the mode in which he uses it show that he depended not so much on Hellenistic sources as on the OT and Jewish apocalyptic writings of the intertestamental period. Its OT roots are found in Hebr *sôd* and in Aram *rāz*, "mystery, secret" (Dan 2:18–19,27–30,47; 4:6). The latter is a Persian loanword, used in Aramaic to designate the revelation made to Nebuchadnezzar in his dreams. QL also offers abundant parallels to the Pauline use of "mystery" (e.g., 1QpHab 7:5; 1QS 3:23), showing that its real roots are in Palestinian Judaism rather than in the Hellenism of Asia Minor. As in QL, "mystery" is a carrier-idea for Paul; it conveys for him the content of his gospel, whereas in QL it conveys the hidden meaning of OT passages.

35   (2) Its *dynamic* nature. Though "the story of the cross" is not recounted by Paul in narrative form, as it is by the evangelists, the gospel for him is not an abstraction. It is "the power of God," a salvific force (*dynamis*) unleashed in the world of human beings for the salvation of all (Rom 1:16). The gospel may, indeed, announce a proposition, "Jesus is Lord" (1 Cor 12:3; Rom 10:9), to which human beings are called to assent, but it involves more, for it proclaims "a Son whom God has raised from the dead, Jesus, who *is delivering* us from the coming wrath" (1 Thess 1:10). It is thus a gospel that comes "not in words alone, but with power and the holy Spirit" (1 Thess 1:5); it is "the word of God, which is at work [*energeitai*] among you who believe" (1 Thess 2:13; cf. 1 Cor 15:2).

36   (3) Its *kerygmatic* character. Paul's gospel is related to the pre-Pauline kerygmatic tradition: "I passed on to you above all what I received" (1 Cor 15:1–2), and he is careful to stress the "form" or the "terms" (*tíni logō*) in which he "evangelized" the Corinthians. In vv 3–5 there follows a fragment of the kerygma itself, and v 11 asserts the common origin of Paul's gospel.

(4) Its *normative* role in Christian life. For Paul the gospel stands critically over Christian conduct, church officials, and human teaching. It tolerates no rival; that there is no "other gospel" (Gal 1:7) is affirmed by Paul in the context of the Judaizing problem in the early churches, when certain Jewish practices were being foisted on Gentile Christians (circumcision, dietary and calendaric regulations). Human beings are called to welcome the gospel (2 Cor 11:4), obey it (Rom 1:5), and listen to it (Rom 10:16–17). It is to be accepted as a guide for life: "Let your manner of life be worthy of the gospel of Christ" (Phil 1:27). Even Cephas, a pillar of the church (Gal 2:9), was rebuked publicly by Paul in Antioch when he was found to be not "walking straight according to the truth of the gospel" (Gal 2:14). Yet for Paul the normative character of the gospel was also liberating, for he mentions "the truth of the gospel" in connection with "the freedom that we have in Christ Jesus" (Gal 2:4), which has to be preserved in the face of the opposition of "false brethren" seeking to undermine it. Hence, though normative, it also liberates from legalisms devised by humans.

(5) Its *promissory* nature. The gospel continues the promises made by God of old: "promised beforehand through the prophets in the holy Scriptures" (Rom 1:1; cf. Isa 52:7). See further Gal 3:14–19; 4:21–31; Rom 4:13–21; 9:4–13. (This characteristic is more fully formulated in Eph 1:13; 3:6.)

(6) Its *universal* character. The gospel is God's power for the salvation of "everyone who has faith, the Jew first and also the Greek" (Rom 1:16; cf. 10:12).

(Bring, R., "The Message to the Gentiles: A Study to the Theology of Paul the Apostle," *ST* 19 [1965] 30–46. Brown, R. E., *The Semitic Background of the Term "Mystery" in the New Testament* [FBBS 21; Phl, 1968]. Fitzmyer, J. A., "The Gospel in the Theology of Paul," *TAG*, 149–61. Friedrich, G., "*Euangelizomai*, etc.," *TDNT* 2, 707–37. Johnson, S. L., Jr., "The Gospel That Paul Preached," *BSac* 128 [1971] 327–40. O'Brien, P. T., "Thanksgiving and the Gospel in Paul," *NTS* 21 [1974–75] 144–55. Schlier, H., "*Euangelion* im Römerbrief," *Wort Gottes in der Zeit* [Fest. K.-H. Schelkle; eds. H. Feld and J. Nolte; Düsseldorf, 1973] 127–42. Strecker, G., "*Euangelizō*" and "*Euangelion*," *EWNT* 2, 173–86. Stuhlmacher, P., *Das paulinische Evangelium: I. Vorgeschichte* [FRLANT 95; Göttingen, 1968]; "Das paulinische Evangelium," *Das Evangelium und die Evangelien: Vorträge von Tübinger Symposium 1982* [ed. P. Stuhlmacher; WUNT 28; Tübingen, 1983] 157–82.)

37   (C) God and His Plan of Salvation History. The nuance of mystery added by Paul to his idea of the gospel opens up a broad perspective: He saw the gospel as part of a plan, gratuitously conceived by God for a new form of human salvation, to be revealed and realized in his Son. The author of this plan was God (*ho theos*, 1 Cor 2:7), whom Paul had worshiped as Pharisee, the God of "the covenants" (Rom 9:4) of old. What Paul teaches about God is not a theology (in the strict sense) independent of his christocentric soteriology, for this God is the "Father of our Lord Jesus Christ" (2 Cor 1:3;

Rom 15:6), and what he says about God is usually asserted in contexts dealing with his salvific activity. "It pleased God to save those who believe through the folly of the gospel message [*kērygma*]" (1 Cor 1:21). Even when Paul speaks of the qualities or attributes of God, they almost always depict God as such and such *for us, on our behalf.* Thus he acknowledges God as Creator: the "one God, the Father, from whom are all things and for whom we exist" (1 Cor 8:6); he is "the living and true God" (1 Thess 1:9); "the God who said, 'Let light shine out of darkness' [cf. Gen 1:3], who has shone in our hearts" (2 Cor 4:6); he is the one who "calls into being what does not exist"—so depicted in Paul's use of the Abraham story (Rom 4:19). Paul speaks of God's "eternal power and divinity" (Rom 1:20), his "truth" (1:25), and his "wisdom and knowledge" (11:33).

38   Three qualities of God, however, have to be singled out in particular. (1) "The wrath of God" (*orgē theou*, Rom 1:18; cf. 1 Thess 1:10; 2:16; 5:9; Rom 2:8; 3:5; 4:15; 5:9; 9:22; [Col 3:6; Eph 5:6]). This quality is inherited by Paul from the OT (see Ps 78:31; cf. Isa 30:27–28), where it expresses not so much a divine emotion as God's reaction to evil and sin. God may seem to be portrayed anthropomorphically with an angry frame of mind, but "the wrath of God" is not meant to express his malicious hatred or jealous caprice. It is the OT way of expressing God's steadfast reaction as a judge to Israel's breach of the covenant relation (Ezek 5:13; 2 Chr 36:16) or to the nations' oppression of his people (Isa 10:5–11; Jer 50 [LXX 28]:11–17). Related to "the Day of Yahweh" (Zeph 1:14–18), wrath was often conceived of as God's eschatological retribution. For Paul it is either already "manifested" (Rom 1:18) or still awaited (Rom 2:6–8).

(Pesch, W., "*Orgē*," *EWNT* 2, 1293–97. MacGregor, G. H. C., "The Concept of the Wrath of God in the New Testament," *NTS* 7 [1960–61] 101–9. Wilckens, U., *Der Brief an die Römer* [EKKNT 6/1–3; Einsiedeln, 1978–82] 101–2.)

39   (2) In contrast to "God's wrath," there stands "the uprightness" or "the righteousness of God," appearing as a quality in Rom 1:17; 3:5,21–22,25–26; 10:3. (In 2 Cor 5:21 it is rather conceived of as a gift given to human beings; cf. Phil 3:9.) This quality of God is also inherited by Paul from the OT, even though the phrase itself is not found as such. The closest one comes to the Pauline phrase is *ṣidqat Yhwh*, "the just decrees of the Lord" (Deut 33:21 *RSV*; cf. LXX, *dikaiosynēn Kyrios epoiēsen*, "the Lord has wrought righteousness") or *ṣidqôt Yhwh*, "the triumphs of the Lord" (Judg 5:11 *RSV*; cf. LXX, *ekei dōsousin dikaiosynas Kyriō*, "there they will grant the Lord righteous acts"). The exact equivalent of the Pauline phrase, however, is found in QL (1QM 4:6, *ṣedeq ᵓEl*), revealing its pre-Christian Palestinian usage. In the early books of the OT *ṣedeq* or *ṣĕdāqāh* expresses the quality by which Yahweh, depicted as involved in a lawsuit (*rîb*) with his rebellious people, judges Israel and displays his "righteousness" (Isa 3:13; Jer 12:1; Hos 4:1-2; 12:3; Mic 6:2). It describes his legal or judicial activity; he judges with "righteousness" (Ps 9:9; 96:13; 98:9). In this context "the triumphs of the Lord" should be understood as his legal triumphs (cf. Mic 6:5; 1 Sam 12:7). At times OT scholars try to claim that Yahweh's righteousness has a cosmic dimension, that creation and all that he has done in the OT may be attributed to this divine quality. Appeal is made to Dan 9:14 or Jer 31:35–36 (see H. H. Schmid, *Gerechtigkeit als Weltordnung* [BHT 40; Tübingen, 1968]; H. G. Reventlow, *Rechtfertigung im Horizont des Alten Testaments* [BEvT 58; Munich, 1971]). To do this, however, they have to empty the quality of its legal or judicial aspect; creation and the regulating of world order are scarcely judicial acts. In the postexilic period, however, *ṣedeq* as a quality of God acquires an added nuance; it becomes the quality whereby he acquits his people, manifesting toward them his gracious salvific activity in a just judgment (see Isa 46:13 [where "my righteousness" and "my salvation" stand in parallelism]; 51:5,6,8; 56:1; 61:10; Ps 40:9–10). Similarly, in the LXX *dikaiosynē* is used to translate other (nonjudicial) covenant qualities of God: his *ʾĕmet*, "fidelity" (Gen 24:49; Josh 24:14; 38:19); his *ḥesed*, "steadfast mercy" (Gen 19:19; 20:13; 21:23)—a mode of translating that reflects more the postexilic nuance of *ṣedeq* than its original denotation. In virtue of this OT understanding of "God's uprightness," Paul sees God providing a new mode of salvation for humanity as justification by grace through faith in Christ Jesus—as a part of his plan of salvation history. E. Käsemann has also insisted on Paul's notion of God's righteousness as his "saving activity" and as a manifestation of God's power: "God's sovereignty over the world revealing itself eschatologically in Jesus . . . , the rightful power with which God makes his cause triumph in the world which has fallen away from him and which yet, as creation, is his inviolable possession" (E. Käsemann, " 'The Righteousness of God,' " 180). This can be said, but once again one must guard against the emptying out of the legal or judicial denotation that is basic to the quality. Käsemann, however, rightly insists on the aspect of "power" in God's uprightness.

(Berger, K., "Neues Material zur 'Gerechtigkeit Gottes,' " *ZNW* 68 [1977] 266–75. Drauch, M. T., "Perspectives on 'God's Rightcousness' in Recent German Discussion," in E. P. Sanders, *Paul and Palestinian Judaism* [→ 11 above] 523–42. Bultmann, R., "*Dikaiosynē Theou*," *JBL* 83 [1964] 12–16. Hübner, H., "Existentiale Interpretation der paulinischen 'Gerechtigkeit Gottes': Zur Kontroverse Rudolf Bultmann–Ernst Käsemann," *NTS* 21 [1974–75] 462–88. Käsemann, E., " 'The Righteousness of God' in Paul," *NTQT*, 168–82. Kertelge, K., "*Rechtfertigung*" *bei Paulus* (NTAbh ns 3; Münster, 1967]. Lyonnet, S., "De 'justitia Dei' in epistola ad Romanos," *VD* 25 [1947] 23–34, 118–21, 129–44, 193–203, 257–63. Schlatter, A., *Gottes Gerechtigkeit* [3d ed.; Stuttgart, 1959] 116–22. Schmid, H. H., "Rechtfertigung als Schöpfungsgeschehen," *Rechtf*, 403–14. Stuhlmacher, P., *Gerechtigkeit Gottes bei Paulus* [FRLANT 87; Göttingen, 1965]. Williams, S. K., "The 'Righteousness of God' in Romans," *JBL* 99 [1980] 241–90.)

40   (3) "The Love of God." Though this divine quality does not appear as often as "God's uprightness," it is an important concept for Paul, pervading the second section of the doctrinal part of Rom. It "is poured out into our hearts" (Rom 5:5; cf. 5:8; 8:31–29; 2 Cor 13:11,13; [2 Thess 3:5]). In virtue of this quality Paul sees Christians chosen as "brethren beloved by God" (1 Thess 1:4). For him it is the basis of the divine plan of salvation history.

> (Levie, J., "Le plan d'amour divin dans le Christ selon saint Paul," *L'Homme devant Dieu* [Fest. H. de Lubac; Théologie 56–58; Paris, 1963–64] 1, 159–67. Romaniuk, K., *L'Amour du Père et du Fils dans la sotériologie de Saint Paul* [AnBib 15; Rome, 1961]. Schneider, G., "*Agape*," *EWNT* 1, 19–29.)

41   That Paul thinks in terms of a divine plan of salvation history can be seen in his references to God's "purpose" (*prothesis*, Rom 8:28; 9:11), or his "will" (*thelēma*, Gal 1:4; 1 Cor 1:1; 2 Cor 1:1; 8:5; Rom 1:10; 15:32), or his "predestination" (*proorizein*, Rom 8:28–30); cf. "the fullness of time" (Gal 4:4); God's "appointed time" (*kairos*, 1 Cor 7:29–32); the period "from Adam to Moses" (Rom 5:14); the meeting of "the ends of the ages" (1 Cor 10:11), the approach of "the day" of the Lord (Rom 13:11–14); "now is the day of salvation" (1 Cor 6:2). In virtue of this plan God chooses or calls human beings to salvation (1 Thess 5:9; Rom 1:16; 11:11) or to glory (Rom 8:29–31). "All this comes from God who has reconciled us to himself through Christ" (2 Cor 5:18).

Not all commentators are sure that Paul speaks in terms of a divine plan of salvation history, despite the elements listed above to support it. S. Schulz (*ZNW* 54 [1963] 104) has maintained that "the Hellenist Luke is the creator of salvation history." That would imply that such a view was not found among NT writers prior to Luke. In reply, however, W. G. Kümmel ("Heilsgeschichte," 434–57) not only reasserted the Pauline view of salvation history but also listed many interpreters of Paul who have recognized this as a valid aspect of his theology (Bultmann, Dibelius, Feine, Holtzmann, and others.). "Salvation history" cannot be applied in a univocal sense to NT writers; Luke and Paul, in particular, have their own views of it. Indeed, in Paul's view of such history, one may ask about the sense in which the first and second stages are "salvific" (if the first was law-less and the second, though under the law that was destined to bring "life" [Lev 18:5], failed to achieve it). Again, though Paul reckons with the meeting of the ages (1 Cor 10:11), the third stage is for him the *eschaton*, even if it is still part of human "history." In any case, the Pauline view of this salvific plan manifests historical, corporate, cosmic, and eschatological dimensions.

42   (1) The historical dimension of the divine plan is seen in its embrace of all phases of human history, from creation to its consummation. Being rooted in the intervention of Christ Jesus in that history "in the fullness of time" (Gal

4:4), it gives that history a meaning that is not otherwise apparent in it. This dimension leads to a periodization of God's plan of salvation. Most likely Paul derived his three-staged view of salvation history from his Jewish education, for it makes sense only against such a background—Paul views human history through Jewish spectacles. The first period was the time "from Adam to Moses" (Rom 5:13–14; cf. Gal 3:17), the law-less period, when human beings did evil indeed, but when there was no imputation of transgressions (Rom 5:13–14). The second period was the time from Moses to the Messiah, when "the law was added" (Gal 3:19; cf. Rom 5:20), when humanity "was imprisoned, held in custody under the law until" it reached maturity (Gal 3:23); then the law reigned, and human sin was imputed as a transgression of it. The third period is the time of the Messiah, of "Christ," who is "the end of the law" (Rom 10:4), when human beings find themselves "justified by faith" (Gal 3:24), which "works itself out through love" (Gal 5:6), "the fulfillment of the law" (Rom 13:10). Paul realized that the time in which he lived followed upon that when warnings were written in the law (such as Exod 32:1–6 or Num 25:1–18), "composed for our instruction upon whom the ends of the ages have met" (1 Cor 10:11). Here the "ends" refer to the last end of the second period and the opening end of the third, that of "the last Adam," or the Adam of the *eschaton* (1 Cor 15:45). Whether Paul's three-staged view of human history is related to a similar division of the world's duration found in later rabbinic tradition (*b. Sanh.* 97b; *b. ʿAbod. Zar.* 9b; *j. Meg.* 70d), as I once held (*JBC*, art. 79, § 41), may be questioned.

43 (2) The corporate dimension of the divine plan is seen in the role played in it by Israel. Privileged of old through God's promises to Abraham and to his posterity, Israel became the chosen instrument by which salvation would reach all human beings: "All nations will be blessed in you" (Gal 3:8; cf. Rom 4:16; Gen 18:18; 12:3). All the divine preparations for the Christ were thus made within the nation of the Jews: "To them belong filial adoption, God's glorious presence, the covenants, the legislation, the temple cult, the promises, the patriarchs, and even the Messiah according to the flesh" (Rom 9:4–5). But though descended from Abraham, Israel (Rom 11:15) rejected Jesus as the Messiah and thereby apparently excluded itself from the salvation offered in Jesus the Christ whom Paul preached. It might seem that the divine plan had failed in its most crucial moment (Rom 9:6). Paul insists, however, that it has not, for this infidelity of Israel was foreseen by God and was part of the plan itself. It is not contrary to God's direction of history, as both the infidelity of the Jews and the call of the Gentiles have been announced in the OT (Rom 9:6–32). Israel's infidelity proceeds from its own refusal to accept him in whom a new mode of uprightness is now open to all humanity. It is only a partial infidelity (Rom 11:1–10), because "a remnant chosen by [God's] grace" (Rom 11:5) has accepted Jesus as the Christ. And it is only temporary, for through Israel's false step "salvation has gone to the

Gentiles to make Israel jealous. But if their false step means riches for the world, and if their failure means riches for the Gentiles, how much more will the addition of their full number mean!" (Rom 11:11–12). Indeed, "only partial insensibility has come upon Israel, to last until all the Gentiles have come in, and then all Israel will be saved" (Rom 11:25). This corporate aspect envisages the effects of the Christ-event on "the Israel of God" (Gal 6:16; cf. Rom 9:6). One must stress this aspect of the salvific plan, for it dominates many passages in Paul's writings, such as Rom 5:12–21; Rom 9–11 (cf. Eph 1:3–12; 2:4–16). It warns us against interpreting Paul's teaching too narrowly or exclusively in an individualistic sense, or as some I-Thou relationship between the Christian and God or, less sophisticatedly, as an individual, personal piety or an exaggerated anthropology. This corporate aspect appears above all in the incorporation of both Jewish and Gentile Christians into Christ and his church.

44 (3) The cosmic dimension of the divine plan is seen in Paul's relating of the entire created *kosmos* to human salvation: "God has put all things in subjection under the feet" of the risen Christ (1 Cor 15:27; cf. Ps 8:7; Phil 3:21). This is why Paul views physical creation itself "eagerly awaiting" its share in the freedom from bondage to decay and in "the glorious freedom of the children of God" (Rom 8:19–21), proleptically attained in the redemption wrought by Christ Jesus. Again, Paul also views the *kosmos* sharing in the reconciliation of sinful humanity achieved by Christ (2 Cor 5:18–21; cf. Rom 11:15). But significantly, he never relates "justification" to this cosmic dimension. (In Col and Eph Paul's disciples develop the cosmic dimension still further in depicting the cosmic role of Christ himself: "All things have been created through him and for him" [Col 1:16]; "that he might be pre-eminent in all things" [Col 1:18; cf. Eph 1:19–23; 2:11–18].)

45 (4) The eschatological dimension of the divine plan is also important, for the first two periods of salvation history (Adam to Moses, Moses to Christ) have been brought to a close, and Christians are already living in the last period. If the *eschaton* has thus been inaugurated, from another point of view the "end" has not yet come (1 Cor 15:24 [according to a most probable interpretation of that verse]). Christ the Lord of the *kosmos* does not yet reign supreme; he has not yet handed the kingdom over to the Father. All this is related to the "Parousia of the Lord" (1 Thess 2:19; 3:13; 4:15; 5:23; 1 Cor 15:23). It is scarcely to be denied that Paul expected it in the near future. However, we find him at times gradually reconciling himself to his own imminent death (Phil 1:23) and to an intermediate phase between his death and his "appearance before the tribunal of Christ" (2 Cor 5:1–10). In either case, there is a future aspect in his salvation history, whether its term be near or far off, and Paul's one hope is "to make his home with the Lord" (2 Cor 5:8), for "to be with the Lord" is the way Paul conceives of the destiny of all

Christians (1 Thess 4:17; Phil 1:23). The undeniable elements of his futurist eschatology are the Parousia (1 Thess 4:15), the resurrection of the dead (1 Thess 4:16; 1 Cor 15:13–19), the judgment (2 Cor 5:10; Rom 2:6–11; 14:10), and the glory of the justified believer (Rom 8:18,21; 1 Thess 2:12). Some commentators would even regard this perspective as "apocalyptic" (E. Käsemann, *NTQT* 133; cf. J. L. Martyn, *NTS* 31 [1985] 410–24; L. E. Keck, *Int* 38 [1984] 234); → 33 above.

But along with this future aspect there is also the present aspect, according to which the *eschaton* has already begun and human beings are already in a sense saved. "Now is the the acceptable time, now is the day of salvation" (2 Cor 6:2). But the "first fruits" (Rom 8:23) and the "pledge" (2 Cor 1:22; 5:5 [Eph 1:14]) are already the possession of Christian believers. Christ has already "glorified" us (Rom 8:30; cf. 2 Cor 3:18; Phil 3:20; [in Eph 2:6 and Col 2:12 this is formulated in terms of Christ having already transferred us to the heavenly realm]). At times Paul speaks as if Christians have already been "saved" (Rom 8:24 [where he adds, "in hope"]; cf. 1 Cor 15:2; 1:18; 2 Cor 2:15); yet at other times he intimates that they are still to be saved (1 Cor 5:5; 10:33; Rom 5:9,10; 9:27; 10:9,13).

This difference of viewpoint is attributable in part to a development of Paul's thought about the imminence of the Parousia. In 1 Thess there are future references; but with the passage of time, and especially after an experience that Paul had in Ephesus when he came close to death (1 Cor 15:32; 2 Cor 1:8) and the Parousia had not yet occurred, his understanding of the Christian situation developed. (This development is further seen in the full-blown vision of the Father's plan that emerges in Col and Eph.)

46 The double aspect of Pauline eschatology has been variously explained. Some, like C. H. Dodd and R. Bultmann, would label the predominant aspect of it as "realized eschatology." This expression is partly acceptable, but care must be had in defining it. For Bultmann, Paul is not interested in the history of the nation of Israel, or of the world, but only in the "historicity of man, the true historical life of the human being, the history of which every one experiences for himself and by which he gains his real essence. This history of the human person comes into being in the encounters which man experiences, whether with other people or with events, and in the decisions he takes in them" (R. Bultmann, *The Presence of Eternity: History and Eschatology* [NY, 1957] 43). In other words, the future elements in Paul's eschatology are only a symbolic mode of expressing human self-realization, as one is freed from self by the grace of Christ and continually asserts oneself as a free individual in decisions for God. In such acts one continually stands "before the tribunal of Christ." Bultmann would thus write off the future elements of Paul's eschatology listed above; they would be vestiges of an apocalyptic view of history, which is meaningless for twentieth-century people. Indeed, he believes that Paul would have already reinterpreted it in terms of his anthropology. "The Pauline view of history is the expression of his view of man" (ibid., 41).

Such an interpretation has the advantage of emphasizing the "critical" moment that the Christ-event brings into the life of everyone. A challenge of faith is presented by it. But this interpretation of Paul's eschatology denies, in effect, some major elements of his view of salvation history. Although truly "the history into which Paul looks back is the history not of Israel only, but of all mankind" (ibid., 40) it hardly seems accurate to say that Paul "does not see it as the history of the nation with its alternations of divine grace and the people's obstinacy, of sin and punishment, of repentance and forgiveness" (ibid., 40). Such a view of Pauline history is too much dominated by the polemics of Rom and Gal and actually minimizes the problem that Paul tried to face in composing Rom 9–11. Israel's history and role in human destiny are factors in Paul's whole theology; they are scarcely theologoumena that one can simply relegate to the realm of myth. Moreover, even if Paul calls Christ "the end of the law" (Rom 10:4), he is not saying that "history has reached its end" (ibid., 43). Rather, he would seem to be saying that a new phase of salvation history has begun because "the ends of the ages have met" (1 Cor 10:11).

47 An alternative to such a "realized eschatology" is to interpret Paul's teaching as an "inaugurated eschatology," or even as a "self-realizing eschatology" (with "self" referring to the *eschaton*). For, in Paul's view, Christians live in the *eschaton*, in the age of the Messiah. This is an age of dual polarity; it looks back to the first Good Friday and Easter Sunday and forward to a final glorious consummation, when "we shall always be with the Lord" (1 Thess 4:17). This age has initiated a status of union with God previously unknown and one destined to a final union with him in glory. This is the basis of Christian hope and patience (Rom 8:24–25).

Such a view of Paul's eschatology reckons with an objective mode of existence in which Christians find themselves through faith, a mode of existence inaugurated by Christ, which will find its perfection in an event that Paul refers to as the Parousia of the Lord. Such an interpretation, however, does not commit one to a naive credulity that fails to reckon with the apocalyptic paraphernalia and stage props used by Paul to describe the forms of the Parousia, resurrection, judgment, and glory—see 1 Thess 4:16–17; 1 Cor 15:51–54 (cf. 2 Thess 2:1–10).

(Allan, J. A., "The Will of God: III. In Paul," *ExpTim* 72 [1960–61] 142–45. Barrett, C. K., *From First Adam to Last* [London, 1962]. Benoit, P., "L'Evolution du langage apocalyptique dans le corpus paulinien," in *Apocalypses et théologie de l'espérance* [LD 95; ed. L. Monloubou; Paris, 1977] 299–335. Dietzfelbinger, C., *Heilsgeschichte bei Paulus?* [TEH ns 126; Munich, 1965]. Dinkler, E., "Prädestination bei Paulus," *Festschrift für Günther Dehn* [ed. W. Schneemelcher; Neukirchen, 1957] 81–102. Goppelt, L., "Paulus und die Heilsgeschichte," *NTS*

13 [1966–67] 31–42. Kümmel, W. G., "Heilsgeschichte im Neuen Testament?" *Neues Testament und Kirche* [Fest. R. Schnackenburg; ed. J. Gnilka; Freiburg, 1974] 434–57. Scroggs, R., *The Last Adam: A Study in Pauline Anthropology* [Phl, 1966].

Baird, W., "Pauline Eschatology in Hermeneutical Perspective," *NTS* 17 [1970–71] 314–27. Longenecker, R. N., "The Nature of Paul's Early Eschatology," *NTS* 31 [1985] 85–95. Mayer, B., "*Elpis*, etc." *EWNT* 1, 1066–75. Gager, J. G., "Functional Diversity in Paul's Use of End-Time Language," *JBL* 89 [1970] 325–37.)

48   (D) Christ's Role in Salvation History. Against the background of the gospel, the mystery, and the Father's plan of salvation, we must now try to depict the role of Christ himself as seen by Paul. For although Abraham and Israel play roles in the execution of that plan and the church is deeply involved in it, Christ's role is central to Paul's thought. Only rarely does Paul refer to "Jesus" solely by his proper name (1 Thess 4:14; Gal 6:17; Phil 2:10; 1 Cor 12:3 [probably a quoted slogan]; 2 Cor 4:5 [see *app. crit.*],10,11,14; 11:4; Rom 8:11), in contrast to an abundant use of titles for Jesus—with one even as his second name (→ 51 below). This immediately indicates the primary interest of Paul in the significance of Christ Jesus, or, in our terms, christology.

49   (a) PREEXISTENT SON. Paul calls Jesus "the son of God" (Gal 2:20; 3:26; 2 Cor 1:19) or "his [i.e., the Father's] Son" (1 Thess 1:10 [in a kerygmatic fragment]; Gal 1:16; 4:4,6; 1 Cor 1:9; Rom 1:3,9; 5:10; 8:3,29,32 ["his own Son"]; [cf. Col 1:13; Eph 4:13]). What did he mean by the title "Son of God"? Given its long history in the ancient Near East, the title could imply many things. Egyptian pharaohs were looked on as "sons of God," because the sungod Rê was regarded as their father (C. J. Gadd, *Ideas of Rule in the Ancient East* [London, 1948] 45–50). Its use is also attested in references to Assyrian and Babylonian monarchs. In the Greco-Roman world it was used of the ruler, especially in the phrase *divi filius* or *theou huios* applied to the Roman emperor (see A. Deissmann, *LAE*, 350–51). It was also applied to mythical heroes and thaumaturges (sometimes called *theioi andres*), and even to historical persons such as Apollonius of Tyana, Pythagoras, and Plato (see G. P. Wetter, *Der Sohn Gottes* [FRLANT 26; Göttingen, 1916]). The basis of the Hellenistic attribution of this title was apparently the conviction that such persons had divine powers. Although some have maintained that the application of this title to Jesus stems entirely from such a Hellenistic background (since it could scarcely have been used by Jesus himself or even applied to him by the early Palestinian community [H. J. Schoeps, *Paul*, 158]), that contention is by no means clear.

50   In the OT, "son of God" is a mythological title given to angels (Job 1:6; 2:1; 38:7; Ps 29:1; Dan 3:25; Gen 6:2); a title of predilection for the people of

Israel collectively (Exod 4:22; Deut 14:1; Hos 2:1; 11:1; Isa 1:2; 30:1; Jer 3:22; Wis 18:13); a title of adoption for a king on the Davidic throne (2 Sam 7:14; Ps 2:7; 89:27); for judges (Ps 82:6); for the upright individual Jew (Sir 4:10; Wis 2:18). It is often said to have been a messianic title, but there is no clear evidence of such usage in pre-Christian Palestinian Judaism; not even Ps 2:7 is clearly to be interpreted as messianic. But "Son of God" and "Son of the Most High" are attested in QL (4Q246 2:1), even if the subject of attribution is lost because of the fragmentary state of the text (see J. A. Fitzmyer, *WA*, 90–94). One also hesitates about the use of "son" in 4QFlor (=4Q174) 1:11, which cites 2 Sam 7:14 in a context that some claim is messianic. See further 1QSa 2:11–12, where God's begetting the Messiah seems to be mentioned (*JBL* 75 [1956] 177 n. 28; cf. J. Starcky, *RB* 70 [1963] 481–505). None of these texts is unequivocal. The identification of the Messiah and the Son of God is made in the NT (Mark 14:61; Matt 16:16), and Cullmann may be right in thinking that the fusion of the two titles "Son of God" and "Messiah" first takes place in the NT in reference to Jesus. The dominant idea underlying the use of "Son of God" in the Jewish world was that of divine election for a God-given task and the corresponding obedience to such a vocation. The Hebraic notion of sonship is at the root of the NT application of the title to Christ.

Paul is scarcely the creator of this title for Christ; he inherits it from the early church. It is found in fragments of the kerygma that he incorporates into his letters (e.g., Rom 1:3, "God's gospel concerning his Son" [see H. Conzelmann, *OTNT*, 77]). But the term does not always have the same connotation. When Paul says that Jesus was "set up as a Son of God in power with a spirit of holiness as of the resurrection from the dead" (Rom 1:4), he uses the title in the Hebraic sense. It expresses the role of Jesus endowed with a life-giving spirit for the salvation of human beings (1 Cor 15:45). Elsewhere Paul presupposes, if he does not allude to, the preexistence of Christ. "God sent his Son, born of a woman, subject to the law, to redeem those who were under the law" (Gal 4:4); cf. "his own Son" (Rom 8:3,32). Theoretically, one could say that this "sending" refers to nothing more than a divine commission. But is that all that Paul implies? The ambiguity seems to be removed by Phil 2:6, "Who, though of divine status" (*en morphē theou hyparchōn*); cf. 2 Cor 8:9. The status that the Son enjoyed was one of "being equal to God" (*to einai isa theō*). (In Col 1:15,17; 2:9 reference is made to Jesus as the Son, who was "the image of the invisible God, the first-born of all creation"). In 1 Cor 15:24–25,28, Paul further speaks of Christ as "the Son" in a way that may even transcend functional christology, for he treats there of the end of the salvific plan, when "the Son himself" will be subjected to him (the Father) who has put all things under his feet. Christ with his role brought to completion is "the Son," related to the Father.

51   (b) CHRISTOS. In the LXX *christos* is the Gk translation of Hebr *māšiaḥ*, "anointed (one)," a title often used for historical kings of Israel (e.g., 1 Sam

16:6; 24:7,11; 26:16), rarely for a high priest (Lev 4:5,16), and once even for a pagan king (Cyrus, Isa 45:1). Because it was often used of David, when the Davidic line was carried off into Babylonian captivity (Jer 36:30) and the promise of a future "David" to be raised up by God emerged in Israel (Jer 30:9; cf. 23:5), the title was eventually transferred to that figure (see Dan 9:25, "to the coming of a Messiah, a prince"). Thus arose the messianic expectation in Israel. The title denoted an anointed agent of Yahweh awaited by the people for their deliverance. This expectation of a coming Messiah developed further among the Essenes of Qumran: "until the coming of a prophet and the Messiahs of Aaron and Israel" (1QS 9:11).

The title was applied to Jesus of Nazareth very quickly after his death and resurrection, evoked among his followers undoubtedly by the title that Pilate had affixed to his cross, "King of the Jews" (Mark 14:26; cf. N. A. Dahl, *The Crucified Messiah*, 23–33; note that the kerygmatic fragment preserved in Acts 2:36 hints at the same application). What is striking about the Pauline use of *Christos* is not its frequency (266 times in his uncontested letters [81 in the Deutero-Paulines; 32 in the Pastorals]), but its having practically become Jesus' second name: "Jesus Christ" (e.g., 1 Thess 1:1,3) or "Christ Jesus" (e.g., 1 Thess 2:14, 5:18). Only in Rom 9:5 does he clearly use *Christos* in a titular sense; even then it is not a generic title but refers to the one Messiah, Jesus. Dahl (*The Crucified Messiah*, 40, 171) would detect "messianic connotations" in the use of *Christos* in 1 Cor 10:4; 15:22; 2 Cor 5:10; 11:2–3; Phil 1:15,17; 3:7; Rom 1:2–4; but each of these instances is debatable. Therefore, what is important is to realize that for Paul *Christos* meant what Christians had come to understand about the former Jewish title. Paul came to faith through "a revelation of Jesus Christ" (Gal 1:12), a revelation in which "the Father revealed his Son to/in me" (Gal 1:16), that he might preach him among the Gentiles. Whereas before the Damascus experience Paul persecuted "the churches of Christ" (Gal 1:22) and their faith in Jesus as the Messiah, the revelation of Jesus as God's Son not only brought an abrupt break with his past but corrected his own messianic belief. That belief became, as it were, second nature to Paul, and the title soon became Jesus' second name.

(Dahl, N. A., *The Crucified Messiah and Other Essays* [Minneapolis, 1974]. Hahn, F., *The Titles of Jesus in Christology* [London, 1969] 136–222. Kramer, W., *Christ, Lord, Son of God* [SBT 1/50; London, 1966].)

52 (c) KYRIOS. Perhaps an even more important Pauline title for Jesus, especially as the risen Christ, is *Kyrios*, "Lord." Paul uses it not as often as *Christos* but more often than "Son" or "Son of God."

Paul employs *Kyrios* for Yahweh of the OT, especially in passages where he quotes or explains OT texts (1 Thess 4:6; 1 Cor 2:16; 3:20; 10:26; 14:21; Rom 4:8; 9:28,29; 11:3,34; 12:19; 15:11; cf. L. Cerfaux, *ETL* 20 [1943] 5–17). In these instances the absolute or unmodified (*ho*) *Kyrios* occurs. Whence comes this absolute usage, even for Yahweh? It is found in the great mss. of the LXX, but they are Christian copies, and *Kyrios* might be the substitution of later Christian copyists. That the usage could have come to NT-era Christians from contemporary Gk translations of the OT is often denied, because "(the) Lord" was an unusual designation for God in Judaism—indeed, according to R. Bultmann, "unthinkable" (*TNT* 1, 51). In Gk translations of the OT made for Jews and by Jews, the tetragram (*YHWH*) was actually written in Hebr characters, or sometimes as *IAO* (see H. Conzelmann, *OTNT*, 83–84). However, there is now evidence that Palestinian Jews in the last pre-Christian centuries were beginning to call their God "the Lord" (absolutely). Thus, Hebr *ʾādôn* is found in Ps 114:7 ("Tremble, O earth, before the Lord, before the God of Jacob"), perhaps also in Ps 151, as it is quoted in 11QPs[a] 28:7–8 ("Who can recount the deeds of the Lord?"—a contested reading; see P. Auffret and J. Magne, *RevQ* 9 [1977–78] 163–88, 189–96). The Aram *mārêh* is found in 11QtgJob 24:6–7 ("Now will God really prove faithless, and [will] the Lord [distort judgment]?" [= MT Job 34:12]). The emphatic *māryāʾ*, "the Lord," occurs in 4QEn[b] 1 iv 5 ("[To Gabriel] the [L]ord said" [= *1 Enoch* 10:9, and the Greek version has *ho Ks*]). Moreover, Gk *Kyrios* is used twice by Josephus (*Ant.* 20.4,2 § 90, in a prayer of King Izates, a convert to Judaism; *Ant.* 13.3,1 § 68, quoting Isa 19:9 in a letter of Onias the High Priest). Such evidence shows that Palestinian Jews, speaking Hebrew, Aramaic, or Greek, were beginning (at least) to refer to God as "the Lord."

53   Paul's absolute use of *(ho) Kyrios* for the risen Christ is often attributed to his Hellenistic background (e.g., W. Bousset, *Kyrios Christos* [Nash, 1970] 119–52; R. Bultmann, *TNT* 1, 124; H. Conzelmann, *OTNT*, 82–84), for the absolute use of *kyrios* is well attested in the Hellenistic world of the Roman Empire (see W. Foerster, *TDNT* 3, 1046–58). In religious texts from Asia Minor, Syria, and Egypt, gods and goddesses such as Isis, Osiris, and Serapis were often called simply *kyrios* or *kyria*. Paul himself was aware of this: Though there are many "lords," yet for us there is only one Lord, Jesus Christ (1 Cor 8:5–6). *Kyrios* was also a sovereign title for the Roman emperor (Acts 25:26, where the *RSV* has added "my," which is not in the Greek). Though denoting primarily the emperor's political and judicial sovereignty, it also carried the nuance of his divinity, especially in the eastern Mediterranean area. When the primitive Christian kerygma was carried out of Palestine, it would have encountered this Hellenistic usage—it is argued—and would have adopted this title for the risen Christ. But this argument needs scrutiny, especially in the light of the evidence for the Palestinian Jewish religious usage presented above.

Paul himself inherited the title from the Palestinian Jewish Christian community in Jerusalem, where "Hebrews" and "Hellenists" (Acts 6:1–6) had already fashioned the credal formula, "Jesus is Lord" (1 Cor 12:3; Rom 10:9), and had probably even made it a kerygmatic proclamation. Indeed, the title forms the climax of the pre-Pauline (probably Jewish-Christian) hymn to

Christ used in Phil 2:6–11: "Let every tongue confess to the glory of God the Father that Jesus Christ is Lord" (retroverted into Aramaic: *wĕkōl liššān yitwaddê dî mārê° Yēšûa° mĕšîḥā° liqār °Elāhā° °abbā°*). (Compare Col 2:6, "You have received by tradition [*parelabete*] Christ Jesus as the Lord.") Even when writing to a Greek-speaking community (1 Cor 16:22), Paul preserves *maranatha*, "Our Lord, come!" a liturgical formula related to *Kyrios*. Though no longer the absolute form, it betrays an early Palestinian origin, for it reflects Aram *māránā° thā°* (cf. Rev 22:20: "Come, Lord Jesus!"; *Did*. 10.6). It was an eschatological prayer invoking the parousiac Lord, probably derived from a eucharistic liturgy considered as a foretaste of that coming (see 1 Cor 11:26). Such evidence suggests, then, that Paul derived the use of "Lord" for the risen Christ from the early Jewish-Christian community of Jerusalem itself.

54   What did the title *Kyrios* mean for Paul? (1) It was a way of referring to the risen status of Jesus the Christ. "Am I not an apostle? Have I not seen Jesus our Lord?" (1 Cor 9:1). So exclaimed Paul in relating his claim to apostleship to his vision of the risen Christ. (2) It expressed for him, as it did for the Jewish Christians before him, that this exalted Christ (Phil 2:9) was worthy of the same adoration as Yahweh himself, as the allusion to Isa 45:23 in Phil 2:10 suggests. (3) Both the use of *maranatha* (1 Cor 16:22) and Paul's interpretation of the eucharist ("As often as you eat this bread and drink this cup, you proclaim the death of the Lord Jesus until he comes," 1 Cor 11:26) seem to suggest that *Kyrios* was originally applied to the parousiac Christ, and then gradually retrojected to other, earlier phases of Jesus' existence. (4) Though in itself *Kyrios* does not mean "God" or assert the divinity of Christ, the fact that Paul (and early Jewish Christians before him) used of the risen Christ the title that Palestinian Jews had come to use of Yahweh, puts him on the same level with Yahweh and implies his transcendent status. He is in reality something more than human. (In this regard, one should recall here that only in Rom 9:5 does Paul possibly call Jesus Christ *theos*, "God," and that is a highly controverted text). (5) The title expresses Jesus' dominion over human beings precisely in his glorious, risen condition as an influence affecting their lives even in the present. It is a title by which Christians acknowledge their relation to Christ as the Lord of "the living and the dead" (Rom 14:9). In acknowledging this lordship, Christians along with Paul admit that they are his *douloi*, "servants" (1 Cor 7:22; cf. Rom 1:1; Gal 1:10).

(In Col and Eph the lordship of Christ, developed as "the mystery of Christ," is further explained. As *Kyrios* of the *kosmos*, he has disarmed "the principalities and powers" [Col 2:15]; in him, the "one Lord" [Eph 4:5], the church finds its unity.)

(Boismard, M.-E., "La divinité du Christ d'après Saint Paul," *LumVie* 9 [1953] 75–100. Cerfaux, L., "Kyrios," *DBSup* 5, 200–28. Conzelmann, H., *OTNT*, 76–86. Fitzmyer, J. A., "*Kyrios, kyriakos*," *EWNT* 2, 811–20; "New Testament Kyrios and Maranatha and their Aramaic Background," *TAG*, 218–35; "The Semitic Background of the New Testament *Kyrios*-Title," *WA*, 115–42.)

55   (d) PASSION, DEATH, AND RESURRECTION. The decisive moment of the divine plan of salvation was reached in the passion, death, and resurrection of Jesus, the Christ. The unity of these phases must be retained in Paul's view of this plan. Unlike the Johannine view, which tends to make of the ignominious raising of Jesus on the cross a majestic elevation to glory (John 3:14; 8:28; 12:34) so that the Father seems to glorify the Son on Good Friday itself (John 12:23; 17:1–5), Paul's view sees the passion and death as a prelude to the resurrection. All three phases make up "the story of the cross" (1 Cor 1:18); for it was the "lord of glory" who was crucified (1 Cor 2:8). Though he was humiliated and subjected to powers controlling this age, Jesus' resurrection meant his victory over them as Lord (Phil 2:10–11; 2 Cor 13:4). "He who died" is also "he who was raised up" (Rom 8:34). Although Jesus' assuming of the "form of a slave" (Phil 2:7), that is, becoming human (2 Cor 8:9), is part of the salvific process, Paul is not interested in it apart from the passion, death, and resurrection. For in the last phases of Jesus' earthly existence, Paul sees Jesus' filial obedience really displayed (Phil 2:8; Rom 5:19). Paul often traces the redemption of humanity to the gracious initiative of the Father, but he also makes clear the free, loving cooperation of Christ in the execution of the Father's plan (Gal 2:20; Rom 3:23). It is "our Lord Jesus Christ who gave himself for our sins to rescue us from the present evil age" (Gal 1:4).

56   The early church recorded the memory of Jesus as the Son of Man who said that he had come not to be served but to serve and to give his life as a ransom for many (Mark 10:45). Paul nowhere alludes to such a saying of Jesus, except perhaps in his use of the eucharistic formula in 1 Cor 11:24. Yet he does emphasize Christ's vicarious suffering and death for humanity. His teaching depends on the early church's kerygma (1 Cor 15:3: "Christ died for our sins"), echoed often in one form or another (1 Cor 1:13, "for you"; Rom 14:15; Gal 1:4; 3:13; 2 Cor 5:14,21; "Christ died for us godless people," Rom 5:6). One may debate whether it should be "for us" or "instead of us"; in either case the basic Pauline idea is present. If at times Paul seems to stress the death of Christ for human salvation (1 Thess 5:10; Gal 2:20; Rom 3:25; 5:6,9–10) without mentioning the resurrection, he does so to emphasize the cost that this experience on behalf of human beings demanded of Christ. "You have been bought for a price" (1 Cor 6:20). Thereby, Paul stresses that it was no small thing that Christ Jesus did for them.

57   At times Paul hints that Jesus' death was a form of sacrifice that he underwent on behalf of human beings. This notion is alluded to in 1 Cor 5:7, where Christ is depicted as the passover lamb. A more specific nuance of "covenant sacrifice" is found in the eucharistic passage of 1 Cor 11:24–25. (For the sacrificial interpretation of the disputed passage in 2 Cor 5:21, see the lengthy discussion of L. Sabourin in S. Lyonnet, *Sin*, 185–296.) R. Bultmann (*TNT* 1, 296) may be right in saying that this view of Christ's death is not characteristically Pauline, but represents a tradition that originated in the early church. (The view is explicitly formulated in Eph 5:2, where it is linked to the love of Christ and where allusions are made to Ps 40:7 and Exod 29:18, "As Christ loved you and gave himself up for you as a fragrant offering and sacrifice [*prosphoran kai thysian*] to God.")

58   What is much more characteristic of Paul is the linking of Christ's death and resurrection as the salvific event. The cardinal text in this regard is Rom 4:25: "Jesus our Lord . . . was handed over [to death] for our transgressions and was raised for our justification." See also 1 Thess 4:14; Phil 2:9–10; 1 Cor 15:12,17,20–21; 2 Cor 5:14–15; 13:4; Rom 8:34; 10:9–10. Most of these texts leave no doubt about the soteriological value of the first Easter. Rom 4:25 is not an empty pleonasm or only an instance of *parallelismus membrorum*. It expresses rather, the double effect of the salvation-event: the wiping away of human transgressions (on the negative side) and the instituting of a status of uprightness (on the positive side). Christ's resurrection was not a purely personal by-product of his passion and death. Rather, it contributed as much as these did in a causal way to the objective redemption of humanity. "If Christ has not been raised, then . . . you are still in your sins" (1 Cor 15:17). That Christian faith may be salvific, human lips must acknowledge that "Jesus is Lord" and human hearts must believe "that God raised him from the dead" (Rom 10:9).

59   Note how Paul speaks of the resurrection. Only in 1 Thess 4:14 does he say that "Jesus died and rose again" (as if by his own power). Elsewhere the efficiency of the resurrection is attributed to the Father, the gracious author of the salvific plan: "God the Father raised him from the dead" (Gal 1:1; cf. 1 Thess 1:10; 1 Cor 6:14; 15:15; 2 Cor 4:14; Rom 4:24; 8:11; 10:9; [Col 2:12; Eph 1:20]). Christ's loving generosity is expressed in his being handed over to death, but God's act of prevenient favor is emphasized when Paul attributes the resurrection to the Father. "By the power of God he is alive" (2 Cor 13:4). Indeed, in Rom 6:4 we learn that the power of "the Father's glory" has brought about Christ's resurrection. This *doxa* exalted Christ to his glorious state (Phil 2:10); this heavenly exaltation is his *anabasis*, his ascent to the Father, just as his death on the cross expressed the depths of his humiliation and his *katabasis*. Like so many others in the early church, Paul saw the resurrection-ascension as a single phase of the glorious exaltation of "the Lord." (In Col 2:15 a disciple of Paul views this exaltation as a triumphant victory-ascent over death and the spirit-rulers of this world. God's "surpassing might and strength" was "exerted in raising Christ from the dead and seating him at his right hand in the heavenly realm, far above all principalities, authorities, powers, and dominions and above every name that could be named . . ." [Eph 1:19–21].)

60   For Paul the resurrection brought Christ into a new relationship with people who had faith. As a result of it he was "set up [by the Father] as the Son of God in power with [lit., "according to"] a spirit of holiness" (Rom 1:4). The "glory" that he received from the Father became *his* power, a power to create new life in those believing in him. At the resurrection he thus became the "last Adam," the first being of the *eschaton* (1 Cor 15:45: "The first man Adam became a 'living being'; the last Adam became a life-giving Spirit"; → 79 below). In virtue of this dynamic principle, Paul realizes that it is not he who now lives, but that the risen Christ lives in him (Gal 2:20). As a "life-giving Spirit," Christ brings about the justification of believers and saves them from wrath on the day of the Lord (1 Thess 1:10). Paul even prays "to know Christ and the power of his resurrection" (Phil 3:10), realizing that the Lord is possessed of a power, derived from the Father, and capable of bringing about the resurrection of Christians.

(Dhanis, E. [ed.], *Resurrexit: Actes du symposium international sur la résurrection de Jésus* [Rome, 1974]. Durrwell, F. X., *The Resurrection: A Biblical Study* [NY, 1960]. Fitzmyer, J. A., " 'To Know Him and the Power of His Resurrection' (Phil 3:10)," *TAG*, 202–17. Feuillet, A., "Mort du Christ et mort du chrétien d'après les épîtres pauliniennes," *RB* 66 [1959] 481–513. Güttgemanns, E., *Der leidende Apostel und sein Herr* [FRLANT 90; Göttingen, 1966]. Luz, U., "Theologia crucis als Mitte der Theologie im Neuen Testament," *EvT* 34 [1974] 116–41. Ortkemper, F.-J., *Das Kreuz in der Verkündigung des Apostels Paulus* [SBS 24; Stuttgart, 1967]. Schade, H.-H., *Apokalyptische Christologie bei Paulus* [GTA 18; Göttingen, 1981]. Schweizer, E., "Dying and Rising with Christ," *NTS* 14 [1967–68] 1–14. Stanley, D. M., *Christ's Resurrection in Pauline Soteriology* [AnBib 13; Rome, 1961]. Tannehill, R. C., *Dying and Rising with Christ* [BZNW 32; Berlin, 1967]. Weder, H., *Das Kreuz Jesu bei Paulus* [FRLANT 125; Göttingen, 1981].)

61   (e) THE LORD AND THE SPIRIT. Before considering the various effects that Paul attributes to what Christ has done for humanity, we must devote some attention to the relation of the Lord to the Spirit in the Father's plan of salvation. We have already seen that Paul called Christ "the power of God and the wisdom of God" (1 Cor 1:24). Like the term "spirit of God," these epithets are ways of expressing God's outgoing activity (cf. Wis 7:25); for the "spirit of God" in the OT, see Gen 1:2; Ps 51:13; 139:7; Isa 11:2; 61:1; Ezek 2:2. It expresses God's creative, prophetic, or renovating presence to human beings or to the world at large; through it God is provident for Israel or the world. Though Paul comes to identify Christ with the power and wisdom of God, he never calls him explicitly "the Spirit of God."

In several places, however, Paul does not clearly distinguish the Spirit from Christ. In Rom 8:9–11 the terms "Spirit of God," "the Spirit of Christ," "Christ," and "the Spirit of him who raised Jesus from the dead" are used interchangeably in Paul's description of God dwelling in the Christian. Related to this ambiguity is the designation of Christ as the "last Adam" since the resurrection, when he became "a life-giving Spirit" (1 Cor 15:45), one "set up as the Son of God in power with [lit., "according to"] a spirit of holiness" (Rom 1:4). Indeed, Paul speaks of a sending of the "Spirit of the Son" (Gal 4:6), of "the Spirit of Jesus Christ" (Phil 1:19), and of Jesus as "the Lord, the Spirit" (2 Cor 3:18). Finally, he even goes so far as to say, "The Lord is the Spirit" (2 Cor 3:17).

There are, however, triadic texts in Paul's letters that line up God (or the Father), Christ (or the Son), and the Spirit in a parallelism that becomes the basis for the later dogma of the three distinct persons in the Trinity (2 Cor 1:21–22; 13:13; 1 Cor 2:7–16; 6:11; 12:4–6; Rom 5:1–5; 8:14–17; 15:30). In Gal 4:4–6 there is a double sending of the "Son" and the "Spirit of his Son," and even though one may at first hesitate about the distinction of the Spirit and the Son here, the text probably echoes the distinct sending of the Messiah and of the Spirit in the OT (e.g., Dan 9:25; Ezek 36:26). Moreover, 1 Cor 2:10–11, attributing to the Spirit a comprehensive knowledge of God's profound thoughts, may even imply its divine character.

62 This double set of texts manifests Paul's lack of clarity in his conception of the relation of the Spirit to the Son. Normally, he uses the "Spirit" in the OT sense, without the later theological refinements (nature, substance, and person). His lack of clarity should be respected; he provides only the starting point of later theological developments.

63 As in his christology, so too in his references to the Spirit, Paul is interested in the functional role played by the latter in human salvation. If Christ opened up to human beings the possibility of a new life, to be lived in him and for God, it is more accurately the "Spirit of Christ" that is the mode of communicating this dynamic, vital, and life-giving principle to human beings.

64 The Spirit is for Paul an "energizer," a Spirit of power (1 Cor 2:4; Rom 15:13) and the source of Christian love, hope, and faith. It frees human beings from the law (Gal 5:18; cf. Rom 8:2), from "the cravings of the flesh" (Gal 5:16), and from all immoral conduct (Gal 5:19–24). It is the gift of the Spirit that constitutes adoptive sonship (Gal 4:6; Rom 8:14), that assists Christians in prayer ("pleading along with us with inexpressible yearnings," Rom 8:26), and that makes Christians especially aware of their relation to the Father. The power of the Spirit is not something distinct from the power of the risen Christ: Christians have been "washed, consecrated, and have become upright in the name of our Lord Jesus Christ and in the Spirit of our God" (1 Cor 6:11).

65   Commentators on Paul have at times tried to distinguish between the "Holy Spirit" (*pneuma* with capital *P*) and the "effects" of the indwelling Spirit (*pneuma* with a small *p*)—see E.-B. Allo, *Première épître aux Corinthiens* (Paris, 1934), 93–94. Should not one at times prefer one meaning to the other? Thus Paul might be providing the basis for the later theological distinction between the created gift (grace) and the uncreated gift (the Spirit). But this distinction is not really Paul's; the Spirit for him is God's gift of his creative, prophetic, or renovative presence to human beings or the world, and it is better left in this undetermined state.

66   Related to the foregoing question is the use of *charis*, "grace." For Paul it most frequently designates God's "favor," the gratuitous aspect of the Father's initiative in salvation (Gal 2:21; 2 Cor 1:12) or of Christ's own collaboration (2 Cor 8:9). Thus it characterizes the divine prevenience in the promise to Abraham (Rom 4:16), in the apostolic call (Gal 1:6,15; 1 Cor 15:10; Rom 1:4), in election (Rom 11:5), in the justification of human beings (Rom 3:24; 5:15,17,20–21). Moreover, it characterizes the dispensation that supersedes the law (Rom 6:14–15; 11:6). But at times Paul speaks of *charis* as something that is given or manifested (Gal 2:9; 1 Cor 1:4; 3:10; 2 Cor 6:1; 8:1; 9:14; Rom 12:3,6; 15:15). It accompanies Paul or is in him (Phil 1:7; 1 Cor 15:10). One may debate whether this is to be conceived of as something produced or not. In any case this last group of texts led in time to the medieval idea of "sanctifying grace." Even though to read this nuance into such Pauline passages would be anachronistic, one must remember that the Pauline teaching about the Spirit as an energizing force is likewise the basis of that later teaching.

(Benjamin, H. S., "Pneuma in John and Paul," *BTB* 6 [1976] 27–48. Brandenburger, E., *Fleisch und Geist: Paulus und die dualistische Weisheit* [WMANT 29; Neukirchen, 1968]. Hermann, I., *Kyrios und Pneuma* [SANT 2; Munich, 1961]. Ladd, G. E., "The Holy Spirit in Galatians," *Current Issues in Biblical and Patristic Interpretation* [Fest. M. C. Tenney; ed. G. Hawthorne; GR, 1975] 211–16. Luck, U., "Historische Fragen zum Verhältnis von Kyrios und Pneuma bei Paulus," *TLZ* 85 [1960] 845–48. Stalder, K., *Das Werk des Geistes in der Heiligung bei Paulus* [Zürich, 1962].

Arichea, D. C., "Translating 'Grace' (*charis*) in the New Testament," *BT*, 29 [1978] 201–6. Berger, K., "Charis," *EWNT* 3, 1095–1102. Cambe, M., "La charis chez Saint Paul," *RB* 70 [1963] 193–207. Doughty, D. J., "Priority of Charis: An Investigation of the Theological Language of Paul," *NTS* 19 [1972–73] 163–80. Potterie, I. de la, "*Charis* paulinienne et *charis* johannique," *Jesus und Paulus* [Fest. W. G. Kümmel; eds. E. E. Ellis and E. Grässer; Göttingen, 1975] 256–82.)

67 **(E) Effects of the Christ-Event.** The term "Christ-event" is a short way of referring to the complex of decisive moments of the earthly and risen life of Jesus Christ. Above we considered three of them, his passion, death, and resurrection; but in reality one should also include Jesus' burial, exaltation, and heavenly intercession, for Paul sees significance in these moments as well. We have already noted how little interest Paul shows in the life of Jesus prior to his passion (→18 above). What was more important for him was this complex of six decisive moments. When Paul looked back at these moments, he realized what Christ Jesus had accomplished for humanity, and he spoke of the effects of that accomplishment (the "objective redemption," as it has often been called) under ten different images: justification, salvation, reconciliation, expiation, redemption, freedom, sanctification, transformation, new creation, and glorification. For each of these images expresses a distinctive aspect of the mystery of Christ and his work. If the Christ-event is conceived of as a decahedron, a ten-sided solid figure, one can understand how Paul, gazing at one panel of it, would use one image to express an effect of it, whereas he would use another image when gazing at another panel. Each one expresses an aspect of the whole. The multiple images have been derived from his Hellenistic or Jewish backgrounds and have been applied by him to that Christ-event and its effects. In each case one has to consider its (1) origin or background, (2) meaning for Paul, and (3) occurrences.

68 (a) JUSTIFICATION. The image most frequently used by Paul to express an effect of the Christ-event is "justification" (*dikaiōsis, dikaioun*). (1) It is drawn from Paul's Jewish background, being an OT image expressive of a relationship between God and human beings or human beings themselves, whether as kings and commoners, or brothers and sisters, or neighbors. But it denotes a societal or judicial relationship, either ethical or forensic (i.e., related to law courts; see Deut 25:1; cf. Gen 18:25). Though Noah is described as "a righteous man" before God (Gen 6:9, said in a pre-Mosaic law context), the *dikaios*, "righteous, upright [person]," came to denote normally one who stood acquitted or vindicated before a judge's tribunal (Exod 23:7; 1 Kgs 8:32). Its covenantal nuance was expressive of the status of "righteousness" or "uprightness" to be achieved in the sight of Yahweh the Judge by observing the statutes of the Mosaic law (see Ps 7:9–12; 119:1–8). The OT also noted constantly how difficult a status it was to achieve (Job 4:17; 9:2; Ps 143:2; Ezra 9:15). Whereas Josephus could imagine nothing "more righteous" than obeying the statutes of the Law (*Ag. Ap.* 2.41 § 293), the Essene of Qumran sang of his sinfulness and sought justification only from God: "As for me, I belong to wicked humanity, to the assembly of perverse flesh; my iniquities, my transgressions, my sins together with the wickedness of my heart belong to the assembly doomed to worms and walking in darkness. No human being sets his own path or directs his own steps, for to God alone belongs the judgment of him, and from his hand comes perfection of way. . . . If I stumble because of a sin of the flesh, my judgment is according to the righteousness of God" (1QS 11:9–12; cf. 1QH 9:32–34; 14:15–16). Here we find an awareness both of sin and of God as the source of human uprightness that is somewhat similar to Paul's ideas, but not yet as developed as his would eventually become. Though Paul, even as a Christian, could look back on his own experience as a Pharisee and assert that "as to righteousness under the law" he had been "blameless" (Phil 3:6), his experience near Damascus impressed him with the sinfulness of all human beings and with the role of Christ Jesus in repairing that situation (see Rom 3:23). (2) When Paul then says that Christ has "justified" human beings, he means that by his passion, death, etc., Christ has brought it about that they now stand before God's tribunal acquitted or innocent—and this apart from deeds prescribed by the Mosaic law. For "God's uprightness" (→ 39 above) now manifests itself toward human beings in a just judgment that is one of acquittal, since "Jesus our Lord was handed over [to death] for our trespasses and raised for our justification" (Rom 4:25). (3) Paul clearly affirms the gratuitous and unmerited character of this justification of all humanity in Rom 3:20–26, which ends with the assertion that God has displayed Jesus in death ("by his blood") "to show forth at the present time that he [God] is upright himself and justifies [= vindicates] the one who has faith in Jesus" (3:26; cf. 5:1; Gal 2:15–21). The process of justification begins in God who is "upright" and who "justifies" the godless sinner as a result of what Christ has done for humanity. The sinner becomes *dikaios* and stands before God as "upright, acquitted." For this reason Paul also speaks of Christ as "our uprightness" (1 Cor 1:30), since through his obedience many are "made upright" (*dikaioi katastathēsontai hoi polloi*, Rom 5:19; cf. 1 Cor 6:11; Rom 5:18). Paul insists on the utter gratuity of this status before God because "all have sinned and fall short of the glory of God" (Rom 3:23). He even brings himself to admit that in all of this "we become the righteousness of God" (2 Cor 5:21), a bold assertion that states that God's righteousness is communicated to us. This is "righteousness from God" (Phil 3:9); it is not our own (Rom 10:3).

69   This effect of the Christ-event was undoubtedly recognized by early Christians even before Paul; at least 1 Cor 6:11 and Rom 4:25 are often looked upon as pre-Pauline affirmations about Christ's role in justification. The distinctive Pauline contribution, however, is his teaching that such justification comes about "by grace as a gift" (Rom 3:24) and "through faith" (Rom 3:25). Though it is unlikely that the Judaizing problem in the early church, which Paul combatted so vigorously, gave rise to this way of viewing the Christ-event, that problem undoubtedly helped Paul to sharpen his own view of the matter.

70 The action whereby God "justifies" the sinner has been the subject of no little debate. Does the verb *dikaioun* mean "to declare upright" or "to make upright"? One might expect that *dikaioun*, like other Gk verbs ending in -*oō*, would have a causative, factitive meaning, "to make someone *dikaios*" (cf. *douloun*, "enslave," *nekroun*, "mortify," *dēloun*, "make clear," *anakainoun*, "renew"). But in the LXX, *dikaioun* seems normally to have a declarative, forensic meaning (G. Schrenk, *TDNT* 2, 212–14; cf. D. R. Hillers, *JBL* 86 [1967] 320–24). At times this seems to be the sense in Paul's letters (e.g., Rom 8:33); but many instances are ambiguous. From patristic times on, the effective sense of *dikaioun*, "make upright," has been used (see John Chrysostom, *In ep. ad Rom. hom.* 8.2 [PG 60.456]; *In ep. II ad Cor. hom.* 11.3 [PG 61.478]; Augustine, *De Spir. et litt.* 26.45 [CSEL 60.199]). Indeed, this sense seems suggested by Rom 5:19, "by one man's obedience many will be made upright" (*katastathēsontai*). Moreover, if E. Käsemann's emphasis on "God's uprightness" as "power" is correct, this sense of *dikaioun* acquires an added nuance, and the OT idea of God's word as effective (Isa 55:10–11) would support it. This debate about the forensic/declarative or effective sense of *dikaioun* has been acute ever since the time of the Reformation. Yet it might be well to recall that even Melanchthon admitted that "Scripture speaks both ways" (*Apol.* 4.72). Cf. B. M. Metzger, *TToday* 2 (1945–46) 562; E. J. Goodspeed, *JBL* 73 (1954) 86–91.

(Betz, O., "Rechtfertigung in Qumran," *Rechtf,* 17–36. Conzelmann, H., "Die Rechtfertigungslehre des Paulus: Theologie oder Anthropologie?" *EvT* 28 [1968] 389–404. Daalen, D. H. van, "Paul's Doctrine of Justification and Its Old Testament Roots," *SE VI,* 556–70. Donfried, K. P., "Justification and Last Judgment in Paul," *ZNW* 67 [1976] 90–110. Gyllenberg, R., *Rechtfertigung und Altes Testament bei Paulus* [Stuttgart, 1973]. Jeremias, J., *The Central Message of the New Testament* [London, 1965] 51–70. Keck, L. E., "Justification of the Ungodly and Ethics," *Rechtf,* 199–209. Kertelge, K., *"Rechtfertigung" bei Paulus* [NTAbh ns 3; 2d ed.; Münster, 1967]. Kuyper, L. J., "Righteousness and Salvation," *SJT* 30 [1977] 233–52. Reumann, J., *"Righteousness" in the New Testament* [Phl, 1982]. Strecker, G., "Befreiung und Rechtfertigung," *Rechtf,* 479–508. Wilckens, U., *Rechtfertigung als Freiheit: Paulusstudien* [Neukirchen, 1974]. Wolter, M., *Rechtfertigung und zukünftiges Heil* [BZNW 43; Berlin, 1978]. Ziesler, J. A., *The Meaning of Righteousness in Paul* [SNTSMS 20; Cambridge, U.K., 1972].)

71 (b) SALVATION. A fairly common way for Paul to express an effect of the Christ-event is "salvation" (*sōtēria, sōzein*). (1) This image is most probably derived by Paul from the OT expression of Yahweh's delivering his people Israel, either as its Savior (*môšiaᶜ*, Isa 45:15; Zech 8:7; cf. Ps 25:5; Mic 7:7) or by "saviors" whom he raises up for them (Judg 3:9,15; 6:36; 2 Kgs 13:5; Isa 19:20). It is, however, not impossible that Paul has been influenced by the use of *sōtēr*, "savior," in the contemporary Greco-Roman world, where Zeus, Apollo, Artemis, or Asclepius were often called *theos sōtēr*, a cultic epithet used in time of need (illness, sea storms, travail). This title was also applied to kings, emperors, and town councils (see H. Volkmann, "Soter, Soteria," *DKP* 5, 289–90). (2) The image expresses deliverance or rescue from evil or harm, whether physical, psychic, national, cataclysmic, or moral. (3) In using it, Paul recognizes that Christians "are being saved" by the cross of Christ (1 Cor 1:18,21; cf. 15:2; 2 Cor 2:15), that is, rescued from evil (moral and otherwise). Strikingly enough, he uses this image, and not "justification," in the very thesis of Rom 1:16, where he identifies "the gospel" as "the power of God for the salvation of everyone who believes." Only in Phil 3:20 does Paul call Jesus *sōtēr*, and he is such as one still "awaited," for although Paul looks on this effect of the Christ-event as already achieved, he realizes that its end result is still something of the future, with an eschatological aspect (see 1 Thess 2:16; 5:8–9; 1 Cor 3:15; 5:5; Rom 5:9–10; 8:24 ["In hope we have been saved"!]; 10:9–10,13). Related to this future is the role of intercession ascribed to the risen Christ in heaven (Rom 8:34). This, too, is why Paul can recommend to the Philippians, "work out your own salvation in fear and trembling" (Phil 2:12), adding, however, immediately, "for God is the one working in you, both to will and to work for his good pleasure" (2:13)—lest anyone might think that salvation can be achieved without God's grace. Likewise related is Paul's insistence that all human beings must one day "appear before the tribunal of Christ so that each one may receive good or evil for what one has done in the body" (2 Cor 5:10; cf. Rom 2:6–11). This future aspect of Pauline teaching has to be kept in mind against the broader backdrop of what God has already graciously achieved for humanity in the cross and in the resurrection of Christ Jesus.

(Noteworthy is the development in Eph, where Christ is again called "Savior" [5:23] and where all the characteristic Pauline terminology associated with justification now appears with salvation: "By grace you have been *saved* through faith; and this is not of your own doing, but it is a gift of God—not because of deeds, lest anyone begin to boast. For we are his workmanship, created in Christ Jesus for good deeds, which God prepared in advance that we might walk in them" [2:8–10]. By the time that Eph is written, the Judaizing problem has abated, and the role of grace and faith has been shifted to more generic salvation. See A. T. Lincoln, *CBQ* 45 [1983] 617–30.)

(Brox, N., "*Sōtēria* und Salus: Heilsvorstellungen in der Alten Kirche," *EvT* 33 [1973] 253–79. Cullmann, O., *The Christology of the New Testament* [rev. ed.; Phl, 1963] 238–45. Dornseiff, F., "Soter," PW 2/III.1, 1211–21. Lyonnet, S., "The Terminology of 'Salvation,'" *Sin*, 63–78. Packer, J. I., "The Way of Salvation," *BSac* 129 [1972] 195–205, 291–306. Schelkle, K. H., "*Sōtēr*" and "*Sōtēria*," *EWNT* 3, 781–84, 784–88.)

72   (c) RECONCILIATION. Another image that Paul uses to describe an effect of the Christ-event is "reconciliation" (*katallagē, katallassein* [Col and Eph use *apokatallassein*]). (1) This image is derived by Paul from his Greco-Roman background, as there is no Hebr or Aram word to express the idea in the OT. The LXX uses *diallassein*, which has the same meaning, about a Levite who became angry with his concubine and went to talk to her "to reconcile her to himself" (Judg 19:3); but the Hebr says "to cause her to return to him" (see *RSV*). Cf. 1 Sam 29:4, where the Hebr reads, "He will make himself acceptable." In Hellenistic Greek, however, the verbs *katallassein*, *diallassein* are found abundantly (see J. Dupont, *La réconciliation*, 7–15). The words are compounds of the root *all-*, meaning "other"; they denote a "making otherwise," both in a secular and a religious sense. In a secular sense, they denote a change in relations between individuals, groups, or nations and pertain to relations in the social or political sphere. They mean a change from anger, hostility, or alienation to love, friendship, or intimacy; feelings may accompany that change, but they are not essential (see Matt 5:23–24; 1 Cor 7:11). In a religious sense, Gk literature uses the verbs of the reconciliation of gods and humans (e.g., Sophocles, *Ajax*, 744). Moreover, 2 Macc 1:5 speaks of God being reconciled to Jews (cf. 7:33; 8:29); and Josephus (*Ant.* 6.7,4 §143) similarly tells of God being reconciled to Saul. (2) When Paul applies this image to the Christ-event, he speaks always of God or Christ reconciling human beings, enemies or sinners, to himself. The initiative is with God, who through Christ brings it about that human sinners are brought from a status of enmity to friendship (see 2 Cor 5:18–19). "If, while we were enemies, we were reconciled to God by the death of his Son, much more, now that we are reconciled, shall we be saved by his life. Not only so, but we also rejoice in God through our Lord Jesus Christ, through whom we have now received our reconciliation" (Rom 5:10–11). (3) What is striking in this instance is Paul's extension of this effect of the Christ-event from human beings to the *kosmos* itself: "In Christ God was reconciling the world to himself" (2 Cor 5:19; cf. Rom 11:15). Reconciliation has not only an anthropological dimension but also a cosmic dimension. (In Col and Eph this effect is further developed in that it is related to the overall cosmic role of the risen Christ [Col 1:20–22, and especially Eph 2:11–19]. The reconciliation is described both "horizontally," in that Gentiles and Jews are brought near as Christians, and "vertically," in that both Gentile and Jewish Christians have been reconciled to God through Christ, who is "our peace.")

This idea of reconciliation is the same as "atonement," when that word is understood rightly as *at-one-ment*. Unfortunately, atonement has often been misunderstood and confused with "expiation" (e.g., by E. Käsemann, "Some Thoughts," 50)—and, worse still, with "propitiation." Reconciliation/atonement has nothing to do per se with cult or sacrifice; it is an image derived from relationships within the social or political sphere.

(Büchsel, F., "*Allassō*, etc.," *TDNT* 1, 251–59. Dupont, J., *La réconciliation dans la théologie de Saint Paul* [ALBO 3/32; Bruges, 1953]. Fitzmyer, J. A., "Reconciliation in Pauline Theology," *TAG*, 162–85. Furnish, V. P., "The Ministry of Reconciliation," *CurTM* 4 [1977] 204–18. Hahn, F., "'Siehe, jetzt ist der Tag des Heils': Neuschöpfung und Versöhnung nach 2. Korinther 5,14–6,2," *EvT* 33 [1973] 244–53. Hengel, M., *The Atonement* [Phl, 1981]. Käsemann, E., "Some Thoughts on the Theme 'The Doctrine of Reconciliation in the New Testament,'" *The Future of Our Religious Past* [Fest. R. Bultmann; ed. J. M. Robinson; NY, 1971] 49–64. Lührmann, D., "Rechtfertigung und Versöhnung: Zur Geschichte der paulinischen Tradition," *ZTK* 67 [1970] 437–52. Merkel, H., "*Katallassō*," *EWNT* 2, 644–50.)

73 (d) EXPIATION. Another effect of the Christ-event is expressed by Paul under the image of "expiation" (*hilastērion*). (1) Despite attempts to relate this image to Paul's Hellenistic background, it has been derived by him from the OT, that is, from the LXX translation of Hebr *kappōret*, the lid made of fine gold erected over the top of the ark of the covenant in the Holy of Holies, which served as the base for the two cherubim of Yahweh's throne (see Exod 25:17–22). *Kippēr* in Hebrew basically means "smear over, wipe away" (see *HALAT*, 470), and the lid was called *kappōret* because it was smeared with sacrificial blood by the high priest who entered the Holy of Holies once a year for this purpose on *yôm hakkippûrîm* (Lev 16:14–20). The first time that *kappōret* occurs in the OT it is translated in the LXX by *hilastērion epithema* (Exod 25:17), "expiating cover/lid," but thereafter simply as *to hilastērion* (e.g., Exod 25:18–22 [where the art. is used, as in the MT]), a noun signifying "means of expiation." In the Latin Vulgate, *kappōret* was rendered in most cases as *propitiatorium* (whence the translation "propitiatory" in some older Eng Bibles). Luther translated it as *Gnadenstuhl*, and in imitation the KJV rendered it as "mercy seat." (2) Paul uses this image as an effect of the Christ-event only in Rom 3:25, where he reflects its OT relation to the Day of Atonement ritual in Lev 16: "God displayed him [Christ] as *hilastērion* with [*or* in] his blood for the remission of bygone sins. . . ." Thus, Christ by his death or the shedding of his blood has achieved for humanity once and for all what the Day of Atonement ritual symbolized each year for Israel of old; he has become the new "mercy seat." *Hilastērion* could, in fact, be understood as an adjective: "displayed Christ as expiating"; but, given the more common use of the noun in the LXX, it is preferably interpreted as a noun, "displayed Christ as a means of expiation," that is, a means whereby human sin is wiped out, smeared away. (3) Some commentators have tried to relate *hilastērion* to the Gk verb *hilaskesthai*, which was often used in the Hellenistic period with a god or hero as its object and meant "to propitiate, placate, appease" such an angry being. This might suggest that Paul was saying that Christ was so displayed with his blood in order to placate the Father's wrath (see L. Morris, "The Meaning"). This is, however, far from certain. In the LXX, God is at times the object of *hilaskesthai* (Mal 1:9; Zech 7:2; 8:22); but in these three places there is no question of an appeasement of his wrath (see the *RSV*). More frequently *hilaskesthai* is used either of expiating sins (i.e., removing them or their guilt, Ps 65:4; Sir 5:6; 28:5) or of expiating some object, person, or place (i.e., purifying from defilement, Lev 16:16,20,33; Ezek 43:20,26; etc.). It frequently translates *kippēr*, which even has God sometimes as its subject, not its object (see S. Lyonnet, "The Terminology of 'Expiation' "). One should not invoke such passages as 1 Thess 1:10 or Rom 5:9 to suggest that the shedding of Christ's blood has actually appeased the Father's wrath; we have explained "the wrath of God" (→ 38 above), and it is reserved for human sin. Expiation, however, wipes away human sin, and Paul sees this achieved once and for all in Jesus' death on the cross.

74 A fuller meaning of the public manifestation of Christ "in his blood" (Rom 3:25) is understood only when contemporary Jewish ideas are recalled that "there is no expiation of sins without blood" (Heb 9:22; cf. *Jub.* 6:2,11,14). It was not that blood shed in sacrifice pleased Yahweh; nor that the shedding of the blood and ensuing death were a recompense or price to be paid. Rather, the blood was shed either to purify and cleanse objects ritually dedicated to Yahweh's service (Lev 16:15–19) or to consecrate objects or persons to that service (i.e., by removing them from the profane and uniting them intimately with Yahweh, as it were, in a sacred pact; cf. Exod 24:6–8). On the Day of Atonement the high priest sprinkled the *kappōret* with blood "because of the uncleanness of the Israelites and their transgressions in all their sins" (Lev 16:16). The underlying reason is found in Lev 17:11: "The life of the flesh is in the blood; for it is the blood that expiates by reason of the life [*bannepeš*]." Cf. Lev 17:14; Gen 9:4; Deut 12:23. Blood was identified with life itself because the *nepeš*, "breath," was thought to be in the blood. When it ran out of a being, the *nepeš* left. The blood shed in sacrifice was not, then, a vicarious punishment meted out on an animal instead of on the person who immolated it. Rather, the "life" of the animal was consecrated to God (Lev 16:8–9); it was a symbolic dedication of the life of the person who sacrificed to Yahweh. It cleansed people of faults in Yahweh's sight and associated them once more with Yahweh. Christ's blood, shed in expiation of human sin, removed the sins that alienated human beings from God. Paul insists on the gracious and loving initiative of the Father and on the love of Christ himself in this action. He often says of Christ that he "gave himself" for us or for our sins (Gal 1:4; 2:20) and that he "loved us" (Gal 2:20; Rom 8:35,37). Through the death of Christ, Paul (along with all Christians) has been crucified with Christ so that he "may live for God" (Gal 2:19). It is *not* Pauline teaching that the Father willed the death of his Son to satisfy the debts owed to God or to the devil by human sinners. Lest Paul's statements, which are at times couched in juridical terminology, be forced into too rigid categories after the fashion of some patristic and scholastic commentators, one has to insist on the love of Christ involved in this activity. Paul did not theorize about the Christ-event, as did later theologians. He offers us "not theories but vivid metaphors, which can, if we will let them operate in our imagination, make real to us the saving truth of our redemption by Christ's self-offering on our behalf. . . . It is an unfortunate kind of sophistication which believes that the only thing to do with metaphors is to turn them into theories" (*RITNT*, 222–23).

(Dodd, C. H., *The Bible and the Greeks* [London, 1935] 82–95. Fitzer, G., "Der Ort der Versöhnung nach Paulus," *TZ* 22 [1966] 161–83. Fitzmyer, J. A., "The Targum of Leviticus from Qumran Cave 4," *Maarav* 1 [1978–79] 5–23. Garnet, P., "Atonement Constructions in the Old Testament and the Qumran Scrolls," *EvQ* 46 [1974] 131–63. Lyonnet, S., "The Terminology of 'Expiation' in the Old Testament . . . in the New Testament," *Sin*, 120–66. Manson, T. W., "*Hilastēr-ion*," *JTS* 46 [1945] 1–10. Moraldi, L., *Espiazione sacrificale e riti espiatori nell'ambiente biblico e nell'Antico Testamento* [AnBib 5; Rome, 1956] 182–221. Morris, L., "The Biblical Use of the Term 'Blood,' " *JTS* 3 [1952] 216–27; "The Meaning of *hilastērion* in Romans iii. 25," *NTS* 2 [1955–56] 33–43. Roloff, J., "*Hilastērion*," *EWNT* 2, 455–57.)

75   (e) REDEMPTION. Yet another image employed by Paul to describe an effect of the Christ-event is "redemption" (*apolytrōsis; agorazein, exagorazein*). (1) It is not easy to say whence this image is derived by Paul. It has been related to sacral manumission of slaves in the Gk world (BAGD 12; A. Deissmann, *LAE*, 320–23: More than 1,000 Delphic inscriptions record that "Pythian Apollo purchased So-and-So for freedom"). That Paul is aware of a social institution of emancipation is clear from 1 Cor 7:21, even though he otherwise counsels Christians to remain "in the state in which one has been called," for a slave is a "freedman of the Lord" (7:20,22). But Paul's Gk vocabulary is notably different from that found in the Delphic inscriptions, where the verb is *priasthai*, "purchase," not the Pauline *(ex)agorazein*, which never appears in sacral-manumission texts. Nor is the freed slave ever considered "a slave of Apollo" or "a freedman of Apollo" (see S. Bartchy, *Mallon chrēsai*, 121–25; S. Lyonnet, "L'Emploi"). The only term used in common is *timē*, "price" (1 Cor 6:20; 7:23). For this reason it is better to explain the background of Paul's image mainly in the light of LXX terminology; there the vb. *apolytroun* is used for the "redeeming" of a slave (Exod 21:8), *apolytrōsis* occurs (Dan 4:34), and the simple forms *lytron*, "ransom," and *lytroun*, "redeem," are found abundantly (e.g., Exod 6:6; 15:13–16; 21:30; 30:12). Paul uses *exagorazein*, "buy," a rare word, never used in the LXX in a context of emancipation of a slave or in extrabiblical texts of sacral manumission. But it is used by Diodorus Siculus (*Hist.* 36.2) for buying a slave (as a possession) and again (*Hist.* 15.7) for setting free an enslaved person by purchase—though *lytron* is not mentioned, such a purchase was in effect a "ransom." (2) When Paul sees "redemption" as an effect of the Christ-event, he acknowledges that Christ's passion, death, etc , were a ransom to set sinners free from bondage and enslavement. Behind the Pauline image lies the OT idea of Yahweh as Israel's *gô'ēl*, "redeemer," the kinsman who had the duty of buying back an enslaved or captive relative

(Isa 41:14; 43:14; 44:6; 47:4; Ps 19:15; 78:35). It referred at first to the freeing of Israel from Egyptian bondage (Deut 6:6–8; Ps 111:9), when Yahweh "acquired" a people as a possession for himself (Exod 15:16; 19:5; Mal 3:17; Ps 74:2); later on, to the return of Israel from the Babylonian captivity (Isa 51:11; 52:3–9). In time, it acquired an eschatological nuance: what God would do for Israel at the end of days (Hos 13:14; Isa 59:20; Ps 130:7–8). (3) Paul never calls Christ *lytrōtēs*, "redeemer" (a term used of Moses in Acts 7:35); nor does he ever speak of *lytron*, "ransom." But he does call Christ "our redemption" (*apolytrōsis*, 1 Cor 1:30). "Through the redemption which is in Christ Jesus" (Rom 3:24), human beings are freed and justified. Though this has already been achieved by Christ, there is still a future, eschatological aspect, for Christians "await the redemption of the body" (Rom 8:23)—even a cosmic aspect, since all "creation" (8:19–22) is groaning in expectation of it. When Paul speaks of Christians as having been "bought for a price" (1 Cor 6:20; 7:23), he is stressing the onerous burden of what Christ did for humanity. He never specifies to whom the price was paid (whether to God or to the devil, as later commentators often theorized).

(In Col and Eph "the forgiveness of sins" [*aphesis hamartiōn*] is related to the effect of redemption [Col 1:14; Eph 1:7]. This effect of the Christ-event is never found in Paul's uncontested letters, unless one argues that *paresis* [Rom 3:25] carries the meaning of "remission," which is not unlikely. Moreover, Eph 1:14 explicitly mentions "the redemption of acquisition," echoing the OT idea; in Eph 4:30 the indwelling Spirit is already a pledge of "the day of redemption.")

(Bartchy, S., *Mallon chrēsai: First-Century Slavery and the Interpretation of 1 Corinthians 7:21* [SBLDS 11; Missoula, MT, 1973]. Bömer, F., *Untersuchungen über die Religion der Sklaven in Griechenland und Rom* [4 vols.; Mainz, 1957–63] 2, 133–41. Elert, W., "Redemptio ab hostibus," *TLZ* 72 [1947] 265–70. Gibbs, J. G., "The Cosmic Scope of Redemption according to Paul," *Bib* 56 [1975] 13–29. Kertelge, K., "*Apolytrosis*," *EWNT* 1, 331–36; "*Lytron*," ibid. 2, 901–5. Lyonnet, S., "L'Emploi paulinien de *exagorazein* au sens de 'redimere' est-il attesté dans la littérature grecque?" *Bib* 42 [1961] 85–89; "Redemptio cosmica secundum Rom 8,19–23," *VD* 44 [1966] 225–42; "The Terminology of Liberation," *Sin*, 79–119. Marshall, I. H., "The Development of the Concept of Redemption in the New Testament," *Reconciliation and Hope* [Fest. L. L. Morris; ed. R. L. Banks; GR, 1974] 153–69.)

76 (f) FREEDOM. Related to the image of redemption is another used by Paul, namely, "freedom" (*eleutheria, eleutheroun*). (1) Though "freedom" sometimes carries the nuance of "redemption/ransom" (→ 75 above), it is more properly related to the Greco-Roman idea of freedom as the social status of citizens in a Gk *polis* or a Roman *municipium* (see *OCD*, 703, 851–52). (The root *eleuthero-* occurs in the LXX, but it is found for the most part in the deuterocanonical and apocryphal Gk writings.) The secular use of the adj. *eleutheros* is found in 1 Cor 7:21–22. (2) Paul applies this image to the Christ-event, meaning thereby that Christ Jesus has set human beings free, has given them the rights of citizens of a free city or state. As a result, "our commonwealth [*politeuma*] is in heaven" (Phil 3:20), and while here on earth we are already a colony of free heavenly citizens. (3) Paul's principle is found in 2 Cor 3:17: "Where the Spirit of the Lord is, there is freedom." That is why he insists with the Galatians: "For freedom Christ has set us free; so stand fast and be not encumbered again with a yoke of slavery" (Gal 5:1). The slavery to which he refers is that of "sin and death," "self," and "the law" (see Rom 5–7; esp. 7:3; 8:1–2). "When you were slaves of sin, you became free for uprightness" (Rom 6:20; cf. 6:18). The allegory of Sarah and Hagar (Gal 4:21–31) teaches that all Christians are children of the "free woman." In his struggle with the Judaizers, Paul became aware of the "false brethren" who had "slipped in to spy out the freedom that we have in Christ Jesus" (Gal 2:4). This effect of the Christ-event also has its eschatological aspect, for it is associated with the destiny of the Christian in "glory" (Rom 8:21). Paul, however, realizes that the Christian has not yet fully achieved that destiny and insists, "You were called to freedom; but do not use your freedom as an opportunity for the flesh" (Gal 5:13a-b). Freedom is not license; but "through love become servants of one another" (5:13c).

(Betz, H. D., "Spirit, Freedom, and Law: Paul's Message to the Galatian Churches," *SEA* 39 [1974] 145–60. Cambier, J., "La liberté chrétienne selon saint Paul," *SE II*, 315–53. Krentz, E., "Freedom in Christ—Gift and Demand," *CTM* 40 [1969] 356–68. Lyonnet, S., "St. Paul: Liberty and Law," *The Bridge* 4 [1962] 229–51. Mussner, F., *Theologie der Freiheit nach Paulus* [QD 75; Freiburg, 1976]. Nestle, D., *Eleutheria: Studien zum Wesen der Freiheit bei den Griechen und im Neuen Testament* [HUT 16; Tübingen, 1967]. Niederwimmer, K., "*Eleutheros*, etc.," *EWNT* 1, 1052–58. Schlier, H., "Zur Freiheit gerufen: Das paulinische Freiheitsverständnis," *Das Ende der Zeit* [Freiburg, 1971] 216–33. Schnackenburg, R., "Freedom in the Thought of the Apostle Paul," *Present and Future: Modern Aspects of New Testament Theology* [Notre Dame, IN, 1966] 64–80.)

77   (g) SANCTIFICATION. Another image used by Paul for an effect of the Christ-event is "sanctification" (*hagiasmos, hagiazein*). (1) Though things and persons were often said in the Gk world to be *hagios*, "holy," or dedicated to the gods (Herodotus, *Hist.* 2.41,44; Aristophanes, *Birds*, 522), Paul's image is mainly derived from the OT. There Hebr *qādôš* and Gk *hagios* were often used to characterize things (e.g., the ground, Exod 3:5; Jerusalem, Isa 48:2; the temple, Isa 64:10; its inner sanctuary, Exod 26:33) or persons (e.g., the people of Israel, Exod 19:14; Lev 19:2; Isa 62:12; priests, 1 Macc 2:54; prophets, Wis 11:1). This term did not express an inner, ethical piety or outward sanctimony, but rather the dedication of things or persons to the awesome service of Yahweh. It was a cultic term that marked off from the secular or the profane such persons or things for this service. (2) For Paul, God made Christ Jesus "our sanctification" (1 Cor 1:30), that is, the means whereby human beings were dedicated anew to God and oriented to serve him with awe and respect. (3) To this status "God has called us" (1 Thess 4:7), and we have been "made holy" or "sanctified" by Christ Jesus (1 Cor 1:2; 6:11) or by his "holy Spirit" (Rom 15:16; cf. 6:22). So true is this for Paul that *hagioi*, "saints," becomes a common designation for Christians in his uncontested letters, except 1 Thess and Gal: They are "called to be saints" (Rom 1:7; 1 Cor 1:2). (As in Job 5:1; Tob 8:15; 11:14; 12:15; Ps 89:6,8, *hagioi* sometimes refers to heavenly beings, angels; it may so appear in Col 1:12; cf. 1QS 3:1; 11:7–8.)

(Balz, H., "*Hagios*, etc.," *EWNT* 1, 38–48. Delehaye, P., *Sanctus* [Subsidia hagiographica 17; Brussels, 1927]. Jones, O. R., *The Concept of Holiness* [NY, 1961]. Procksch, O., and K. G. Kuhn, "*Hagios*, etc." *TDNT* 1, 88–115. Wolff, R., "La sanctification d'après le Nouveau Testament," *Positions luthériennes* 3 [1955] 138–43.)

78 (h) TRANSFORMATION. Another effect of the Christ-event is presented by Paul under the image of "transformation" (*metamorphōsis, metamorphoun* [he uses only the verb]). (1) This image is derived from Greco-Roman mythology, which even developed in Hellenistic times a literary form, namely, collections of legends about transformation—of snakes into stones (Homer, *Iliad* 2. 319), of Niobe into a rock on Mt. Sipylon (Pausanias 1.21,3), of Lucian into an ass (Apuleius, *Golden Ass*); cf. Nicander, *Heteroioumena;* Ovid, *Metamorphoses*. This mythological image was quite current in Paul's day, and he did not hesitate to borrow it and apply it to the Christ-event. (2) In so doing, Paul sees Christ Jesus gradually reshaping human beings "who turn to the Lord." The creator God through the risen Christ shines creative light anew in human lives, which transforms them. (3) Paul clearly uses this image in 2 Cor 3:18: "All of us, with unveiled face, behold the glory of the Lord and are being transformed into a likeness of him from one degree of glory to another." Related to this verse is 2 Cor 4:6, which explains how the face of the risen Christ acts as a mirror to reflect the glory that comes from the creator God: "It is the God who said, 'Let light shine out of darkness,' who has shone in our hearts to give us the light of the knowledge of God's glory on the face of Christ." This is one of the most sublime Pauline descriptions of the Christ-event. Phil 3:21 uses another verb, *metaschēmatizein*, to express a similar idea: "Christ Jesus . . . will change our lowly body to be like his glorious body." Cf. Rom 12:2 (in a hortatory context). (From this image Gk patristic writers derived the later idea of *theōsis* or *theopoiēsis*, the gradual "divinization" of the Christian— their practical equivalent for "justification.")

(Behm, J., "*Metamorphoō*," *TDNT* 4, 755–59. Fitzmyer, J. A., "Glory Reflected on the Face of Christ (2 Cor 3:7–4:6) and a Palestinian Jewish Motif," *TS* 42 [1981] 630–44. Hermann, R., "Über den Sinn des *morphousthai Christon en hymin* in Gal. 4,19," *TLZ* 80 [1955] 713–26. Liefeld, W. L., "*Metamorphoō*," *NIDNTT* 3, 861–64. Nützel, J. M., "*Metamorphoō*," *EWNT* 2, 1021–22.)

79 (i) NEW CREATION. Another Pauline image, related to the foregoing, is "new creation" (*kainē ktisis*). (1) Paul has derived this image from the OT references to God's creation of the world and of human beings (LXX Gen 14:19,22; Ps 89:48; 104:1–30; Sir 17:1). (2) In applying it to the Christ-event, Paul means that God in Christ has created humanity anew, giving it "newness of life" (Rom 6:4), that is, a life in union with the risen Christ (Gal 2:20: "Christ lives in me"), a life destined to share in "the glory of God" (Rom 3:23b). (3) "New creation" is found in Gal 6:15, where its worth is contrasted with circumcision and the lack of circumcision; and in 2 Cor 5:17, where its source is "being in Christ." This is why Paul calls the risen Christ "the last Adam" (1 Cor 15:45), that is, he has become the Adam of the *eschaton* through his life-giving Spirit. He is thus the head of a new humanity, just as the first Adam was the beginning of life for physical humanity. For this reason too Christ is "the first-born among many brethren" who have been "predestined to be conformed to his image" (Rom 8:29)—the newness of life that Christ has brought is a share in his own risen life (1 Cor 6:14; 2 Cor 4:14; Rom 6:4–5; 8:11). This is, in effect, the Pauline sense of "eternal life" (Gal 6:8; Rom 5:21; 6:23).

(Baumbach, G., "Die Schöpfung in der Theologie des Paulus," *Kairos* 21 [1979] 196–205. Foerster, W., "*Ktizō*, etc.," *TDNT* 3, 1000–35, esp. 1033–35. Petzke, O., "*Ktizō*, etc.," *EWNT* 2, 803–8. Sjöberg, E., "Neuschöpfung in den Toten-Meer-Rollen," *ST* 9 [1955] 131–36. Stuhlmacher, P., "Erwägungen zum ontologischen Charakter der *kainē ktisis* bei Paulus," *EvT* 27 [1967] 1–35.)

80 (j) GLORIFICATION. The last image used by Paul to describe an effect of the Christ-event is "glorification" (*doxa, doxazein*). (1) This image is derived by him from the OT *kābôd* or *doxa*, "glory, splendor," an expression of the presence of God or of the resplendent manifestation of that presence, especially in the theophanies of the exodus (e.g., Exod 24:17; 40:34; Num 14:10; Tob 12:15). (2) We have already seen how Paul related "glory" to the creator God (→ 78 above); he is now playing on another aspect of that transforming power of the risen Christ. It is depicted as "glorifying" Christians, that is, giving them in advance a share in the glory that he, as one raised from the dead, now enjoys with the Father. (3) Paul speaks of this effect in Rom 8:30: "Those whom he predestined he also called; and those whom he called he also justified; and those whom he justified he also glorified" (*edoxasen*). Cf. 1 Thess 2:12; 1 Cor 2:7; Rom 8:18,21. (In the

Deutero-Paulines this idea is given another formulation: "God has transferred us to the kingdom of his Son" [Col 1:13]; "he has raised us up with him and made us sit with him in the heavenly places" [Eph 2:6]. "Buried with him in baptism . . . you were also raised with him through faith in the action of God who raised him from the dead" [Col 2:12]. "You have been raised with Christ" [Col 3:1]. In none of these Deutero-Pauline passages does *doxa* occur.)

(Brockington, L. H., "The Septuagintal Background of the New Testament Use of *Doxa*," *Studies in the Gospels* [Fest. R. H. Lightfoot; ed. D. E. Nineham; Oxford, 1957] 1–8. Dupont, J., "Le chrétien, miroir de la gloire divine d'après II Cor., III, 18," *RB* 56 [1949] 392–411. Forster, A. H., "The Meaning of Doxa in the Greek Bible," *ATR* 12 [1929–30] 311–16. Hegermann, H., "*Doxa*," and "*Doxazō*," *EWNT* 1, 832–41, 841–43. Schlier, H., "Doxa bei Paulus als heilsgeschichtlicher Begriff," *SPC* 1, 45–56.)

81 **(II) Paul's Anthropology. (A) Humanity before Christ.** What effect does the Christ-event actually have on the lives of human beings? Having sketched the objective aspects of Christ's salvific role, we now discuss the ways in which Paul saw humanity sharing in the effects listed above. To understand his view of the Christian experience from the human side, however, we must inquire first into the way he regarded the human condition prior to Christ's coming. Paul's anthropology (his teaching about humanity) is at once individual and corporate; we sketch the latter first because it is more closely related to salvation history than his view of the individual. For Paul often contrasts what the situation of humanity was with what it is "now" in the Christian dispensation (see Gal 4:8–9; 1 Cor 6:11; Rom 3:21; 6:22; 7:6).

82 (a) SIN. In the period before Christ, human beings were all sinners who, despite their striving to live uprightly, never achieved that goal and never reached the destiny of glory intended by the creator for them; they failed to "hit the mark," as the basic meaning of *hamartanein*, "to sin," implies (see Rom 3:23; cf. 3:9,20). In his teaching on this pervasive influence of sin in humanity, Paul depends on the OT itself (Gen 6:5; 1 Kgs 8:46; Isa 64:5–7; Job 4:17; 15:14–16; Qoh 7:20; Sir 8:5). The tendency to sin is with one from birth: "I was brought forth in iniquity; in sin my mother conceived me" (Ps 51:5; cf. Jer 16:12). Human sin is contagious; the people of Judah "have followed their own hearts in stubbornness and have gone after the Baals, as their fathers taught them" (Jer 9:14; cf. 3:25). Such sin creates a solidarity of sinners, of contemporaries (Gen 11:1–9; 2 Sam 24:1–17; Num 16:22), and of successive generations (Ps 79:8; Exod 20:5; 34:7). This conviction about the universality of sin among human beings was born of experience, observation, and corporate attestation: "No one has power to retain the spirit (i.e., not to die) or authority over the day of death; there is no relief from war, and wickedness will not deliver those who are given to it. All this I have observed, in applying my mind to all that is done under the sun" (Qoh 8:8–9; cf. 7:29). See further 1QH 4:29–30; Philo, *De vita Mos.* 2.29 §147.

83   The etiological narrative of Gen 2–3 sought to explain how this sinful condition began. Its rich symbolism portrays ʾ*Adām*, "Man," and *Ḥawwāh*, "Eve" (explained as ʾ*ēm kol ḥay*, "mother of all living [beings]") as having brought sin into the world. The story teaches that sin did not originate with God, but began with human beings and that it has been around as long as humans have. Through it they lost their trusted intimacy with God and incurred death and all human misery (hard labor, pangs of travail, experience of evil). The cursing of the serpent symbolizes the lasting enmity that is to ensue between humanity and all evil. The notion of inheritance of such a condition through the centuries is introduced in that the woman's offspring will always be confronted by evil; generation after generation of human beings will be seduced by the temptation to become like God, as were their forebears, Adam and Eve.

84   Strikingly enough, this etiological story has produced almost no echo in any protocanonical book of the OT. In these books Adam appears only in the opening genealogy of 1 Chr 1:1. In the so-called Lament over the King of Tyre (Ezek 28:11–19) an allusion to Gen 3 is clear, but Adam is not named, and the transgression is identified as violence-filled "abundance of trade" (28:16), not the eating of fruit. Cf. Job 15:7. Only in the late deuterocanonical books and in intertestamental literature does the story of Eden reemerge, with notable emphases. In Tob 8:6 allusion is made to the creation of Adam and Eve as the origin of humanity; they are looked upon as models of married life. In Sir 36(33):10 the creation of "all human beings" is related to the creation of Adam from the dust. In Sir 40:1 the author alludes to the yoke of heavy toil laid on the children of Adam, and in Sir 49:16 the Hebr text speaks explicitly of "Adam's glory," as he is listed among the "famous men" of old (Sir 44:1). In contrast to this benign treatment of Adam stands Sir 25:24, "Sin began with a woman, and because of her we all die." The origin of sin is traced to Eve, and a causal connection is asserted between it and all human death. Death affects all her descendants because of what she did. Similarly, in *Jub.* 2–5 the story of Gen 2–3 is embellished, and two details are noteworthy: (1) at Adam's expulsion from Eden "the mouth of all beasts was closed . . . so that they could no longer speak" (*Jub.* 3:28); and (2) the depravity of humanity that develops is traced not to Adam's transgression, but to the daughters of mankind seduced by the angels (*Jub.* 5:1–4). The blessings bestowed by God on Adam are later recalled (*Jub.* 19:27), as he is singled out and regarded as one of the patriarchs of Israel. In Wis, Adam is not named, but he is clearly referred to as "child of the earth, the first-formed" (Wis 7:1). Indeed, Wisdom herself "protected the first-formed father of the world, . . . delivered him from his transgression, and gave him strength to rule over all things" (10:1–2). In this late pre-Christian Jewish literature there is thus the tendency to exalt Adam and to trace "the glory of Adam" (1QS 4:22–23; CD 3:20–4:2; 1QH 17:13–15; cf. 4QPs^a 1,3–4 iii 1–2) to his having been created (according to the P document of Gen 1:27) in the image of God. "God created man for incorruption and made him the image of his own eternity, but through the devil's envy death came into the world" (Wis 2:23–24). But whereas Adam is thus extolled, sin, death, and evil are traced to Eve: "I created for him a wife that death should come to him by his wife" (*2 Enoch* 30:17); "Adam said to Eve, 'What have you done to us in bringing on us the great wrath [death], which rules over our whole race?' " (*Apoc. Mos.* 14). Cf. *Apoc. Mos.* 32:1; *2 Esdr.* 3:7. In this late literature only the *Life of Adam and Eve* 44:2 may ascribe the "transgression and sin of all our generations" to "our parents" (in the plural).

85 Paul, however, breaks with this late pre-Christian Jewish tradition about Adam's glory and returns to the earlier tradition of Gen 2–3 itself, ascribing not only death to Adam, but even sin itself. In 1 Cor 15:21–22 he ascribes death to "one man": "As in [*or* through] Adam all die, so too all shall be made alive in Christ." In that context death is contrasted with resurrection to life (eternal), and Paul is thus thinking of total death, spiritual as well as physical. However, in Rom 5:12 he goes further, ascribing to Adam a causal connection that brings not only death, but sin itself into human life: "Just as through one man Sin entered the world, and through that Sin, Death, and in this way Death spread to all human beings, since all have sinned." There follows a notorious anacoluthon because of a break in Paul's thought, as he feels obliged to explain his ascription of *sin* to Adam. Thus Paul attributes to Adam not only the condition of total death that affects every human being, but even the contagion of sin that is ratified by personal sins. This sense of Rom 5:12 does not depend on the vb. *hēmarton*, "have sinned," being understood of some "habitual" sin, or on the prep. phrase *eph' hō* understood as connoting some incorporation of all human beings in Adam. Rather, the context of vv. 13–14 indicates such a causal connection, and especially 5:19, "Just as through one man's disobedience the mass of mankind were made sinners, so by one man's obedience will the mass of them be made upright." The contrast of antitype and type, Christ and Adam, demands that the sinful condition of all human beings be attributable to Adam, just as their condition of uprightness is attributable to Christ alone.

86 Paul's indictment of the ungodliness and wickedness of Gentiles, who have suppressed the truth in their lives, is severe (Rom 1:18–23). He finds that they have no excuse for not honoring God as a result of what they have known about him from his creation (apart from his revelation of himself in the OT). "In not knowing God," the Gentiles "were in bondage to beings that were no gods . . . and were slaves to elemental spirits" (Gal 4:8–9). Their condition of servitude did not enlighten them about their degraded conduct (Rom 1:24–32; cf. 1 Cor 6:9–10). But the picture is not entirely black, for Paul admits that Gentiles do at times fulfill some prescriptions of the Mosaic law (Rom 2:14), "being a law unto themselves," that is, being aware through their consciences of some of what the Mosaic law positively prescribed for the Jews.

87   As for the Jews, who gloried in the possession of the Mosaic law as a manifestation of Yahweh's will and as a guide for their conduct (Rom 2:17–20; 3:2), Paul's indictment of them is equally telling. They may have the law, but they do not keep it (Rom 2:21–24). Not even their practice of circumcision or their possession of the oracles of salvation can save them from the wrath befitting sin (Rom 3:3–8). Without the gospel the entire human race, "all, both Jews and Greeks, are under the power of sin" (Rom 3:9). They find themselves in a condition of hostility toward God (2 Cor 5:19; Rom 5:10; 8:5–7), being dedicated neither to his honor and service (Rom 1:18) nor to honoring his name (Rom 2:24). (In the Deutero-Paulines their condition is depicted as an estrangement from God and bondage to Satan [Eph 2:2; 6:11–12; Col 1:13], which is a form of "death" [Eph 2:1.5; Col 2:13].)

88   Paul refers at times to sin in such a way that one might consider it a "debt" to be remitted (*paresis*, Rom 3:25), but more frequently he treats it as a force or power that has invaded human beings and is abetted by all their natural and fleshly inclinations. The individual wrongful deeds of human beings are "transgressions" (Gal 3:19; Rom 2:23; 4:15), "trespasses" (Gal 6:1; Rom 5:15–18,20), "sins" (*hamartēmata*, Rom 3:25). But Paul often personifies both Death and Sin, depicting them as actors on the stage of human history. *Hamartia* is thus an active evil force that pervades human existence. It "dwells" in humanity (Rom 7:17,23), deceives humanity and kills it (Rom 7:11).

(Barosse, T. A., "Death and Sin in Saint Paul's Epistle to the Romans," *CBQ* 15 [1953] 438–59. Fiedler, P., "*Hamartia*, etc.," *EWNT* 1, 157–65. Lyonnet, S., and L. Sabourin, *Sin*, 3–30, 46–57. Malina, B. J., "Some Observations on the Origin of Sin in Judaism and St. Paul," *CBQ* 31 [1969] 18–34. Weder, H., "Gedanken zu einem qualitativen Sprung im Denken des Paulus," *NTS* 31 [1985] 357–76.)

89   (b) THE LAW AND THE SPIRITS. The human condition before Christ was not only bondage to Sin and Death, but also an enslavement to the "spirits" of this world and to the law. Paul writes to former pagans of Galatia, "In not knowing God, you were enslaved to beings that were no gods" (Gal 4:8). It is debated whether these "gods" are to be identified with the "weak and beggarly elements" (4:9), the "elements of the world" (4:3), often interpreted as spirits controlling the world-elements. See also 1 Cor 2:12. Paul further envisages the possibility of "angels" or "principalities" being hindrances to the love of God poured out on our behalf in Christ Jesus (Rom 8:38–39) or as announcing another gospel different from that which he preached (Gal 1:18). Indeed, angels are conceived of as promulgators of the law of Moses, which held humans in bondage; they thus symbolize its inferiority to the promises that God himself made to the patriarchs of old (Gal 3:19). For Paul such beings were not always evil; they may have been good or at least neutral (1 Cor 11:10, Gal 4:14). Yet if they have held sway over humanity until now, their rule has been broken by the coming of the *Kyrios*, Jesus Christ, because of whom Christians are even to judge the angels (1 Cor 6:3). Paul speaks of Satan a few times (e.g., 2 Cor 11:14; 12:7), in contexts related to his own personal experience of opposition or suffering. He never speaks of the Devil. (In this regard one notes a significant difference in the Deutero-Paulines: Christ's cosmic role includes a victor's place over all "thrones, dominations, principalities, and authorities" [Col 1:16; Eph 1:21], the "elements of the world" [Col 2:20]—or "whatever title is given to them" [Eph 1:21]. Whereas the sinful condition of former pagans resulted from a following of the "course of this world, the prince of the power of air, and the spirit at work in the children of disobedience" [Eph 2:2], Christians are now exhorted to put on the armor of God to stand firm against the wiles of the Devil, because they "are contending, not with flesh and blood, but with principalities, powers, the world-rulers of the present darkness, and evil spiritual hosts" [Eph 6:12]. Such a view is scarcely envisaged in Paul's uncontested letters.)

90 For Paul, however, human beings, especially Israel of old, were also enslaved to the law (Gal 3:23–24). Paul's attitude toward the law (*nomos*) has been called "the most intricate doctrinal issue in his theology" (H. J. Schoeps, *Paul*, 168). His discussion of it is restricted to Gal, Phil, 1–2 Cor, and Rom (in the Deutero-Paulines, reference to it is made only in Eph 2:15, where it is said to be "abolished"). Yet even in these few letters, which reflect the Judaizing problem that confronted Paul, *nomos* carries different connotations. (1) At times Paul uses it in a generic sense, "a law" (Gal 5:23, "against such [fruits of the Spirit] there is no law"; Rom 4:15b, "where there is no law, there is no transgression"; 5:13, "sin is not counted where there is no law"; 7:1a, "to those who know what law is" [?]). (2) Sometimes he uses *nomos* in a figurative sense: as a "principle" (Rom 3:27a; 7:21,23a), as a way of referring to "sin" (Romans 7:23c,25b) or "sin and death" (Rom 8:2b), as "human nature" (Rom 2:14d); indeed, even as a way of referring to "faith" (Rom 3:27b) or to "Christ" (Gal 6:2), or to the "Spirit" (Rom 8:2a)—speaking in the last three instances with oxymoron. (3) On a few occasions Paul uses *nomos* when he refers to the OT, either the Psalms (Rom 3:19a), the Prophets (1 Cor 14:21), or especially the *Tôrāh* (Gal 3:10b; 1 Cor 9:9, the only place where he speaks of "the law of Moses"; 14:34[?]; Rom 3:31b). (4) As for the rest, about 97 times in all, he uses *nomos* (with or without the article) to refer to the law of Moses (cf. R. Bultmann, *TNT* 1, 259–60).

91   In discussing Paul's attitude toward the law of Moses, one has to recall his three-staged view of human history (→14,42 above), perceived through solely Jewish spectacles. He sees it as a stage on which certain figures perform as actors. Among these struts *Anthrōpos*, "Human Being" (Rom 7:1), also called at times *Egō*, "I" (Rom 7:9), confronted not only by *Hamartia*, "Sin," *Thanatos*, "Death" (Rom 5:12), and *Nomos* (Rom 7:1), all personified as actors, but also by *Charis*, "Grace" (Rom 5:21). The roles of these figures come from Paul's own personification of them, attributing to them human acts: They "enter," they "dwell," they "reign," they "revive," etc.

92   The intricate role that *Nomos* plays brings an anomaly into human life. As an actor on the stage of human life, *Nomos* is depicted as good: "The law is holy; the commandment is holy, upright, and good" (Rom 7:12), "noble" (*kalos*, 7:16), and "spiritual" (7:14), that is, belonging to the sphere of God and not to that of this-worldly humanity. For it is "the law of God" (7:22,25b; 8:7), having come from him and destined to lead *Anthrōpos* to "life," that is, to communion with God (7:10). In Gal 3:12, Paul even quotes Lev 18:5, constrained to admit that it formulates the purpose of the law: "the one who does them (i.e., the law's prescriptions) shall live by them," that is, find "life" through them. Again, in Rom 9:4, Paul concedes that the giving of the law was one of the prerogatives of Israel, privileged by God with this means of knowing his will. It was addressed by God to all those who are under its authority and acknowledge it (Rom 3:19). Even when human beings reject the law, it continues to be good, for it is in a sense "God's oracles" (Rom 3:2), entrusted to privileged Israel. Despite this God-given aid whereby Israel might find "life," Paul recognized that his "kinsmen by race" (Rom 9:3) were as much sinners as the law-less Gentiles (Rom 2:17–24 and 1:18–32), for "all have sinned and fall short of the glory of God" (Rom 3:23). Given this situation, Paul formulates the anomaly that the law creates in human life, boldly stating it when he quotes Ps 143:2 and makes a daring addition to it: "No human being shall be justified in the sight of God—*by observing the law*," lit., "by the deeds of the law." Whereas *Nomos* was supposed to lead *Anthrōpos* to life, as Lev 18:5 had promised, it proved incapable of doing so. Thus Paul states the *negative* role of the law in human history: "what the law could not do" (*to adynaton tou nomou*, Rom 8:3). It was incapable of giving life because it was an external norm expressing only do's and don'ts and possessed itself of no life-giving force.

93   Paul went still further in depicting *Nomos* playing a *positive* role in human history. Arriving on the stage in the second act (from Moses to the

Messiah), when it "was added" to the promises already made to Abraham in the first act, it is said to have been added "for the sake of transgressions" (Gal 3:19). "The law came in to increase transgression" (Rom 5:20). Though good in itself, it entered the scene to become the henchman or tool of another actor, *Hamartia.* The law thus became instead the very "force of sin" itself (1 Cor 15:56). Because the law supplied no *dynamis,* "force," whereby *Anthrōpos* could find life in obeying it, it ironically became the instrument of Sin, thus unleashing God's wrath on humanity. "For the law brings wrath" (Rom 4:15). Not sinful in itself, it aided sin: "What then shall we say? That the law is sin? By no means! Yet if it had not been for the law, I would not have known sin," because "in the absence of law sin was dead" (Rom 7:7-8). Paul depicts this positive role of the law as played in three ways.

94   (1) The law acted as an occasion (*aphormē*) for sin, instructing humanity in the material possibility of doing evil, either by forbidding what was indifferent (e.g., the eating of certain animals, Lev 11:2-47; Deut 14:4-21—cf. 1 Cor. 8:8) or by arousing desires or annoying the conscience with external regulations about "forbidden fruit." Paul speaks of this role in Rom 7:5,8,11: The *Egō* would not have known "what it is to covet, if the law had not said, 'You shall not covet' " (7:7).

(2) The law also acted as a moral informer; it gave humanity "a real knowledge of sin" (*epignōsis hamartias,* Rom 3:20), that is, it revealed the true character of moral disorder as a rebellion against God, as a transgression of his will, and as an infidelity to the covenant with its stipulated regulations (e.g., the Decalogue). Paul admits, indeed, that "sin was in the world before the law was given; but sin is not registered where there is no law" (Rom 5:13). He would not have denied that human beings were evil during the first period, from Adam to Moses, but in that law-less period their sins were not booked against them as open rebellion or transgression. Human beings had sinned, but it was not "like the transgression of Adam" (Rom 5:14), who had violated a command of God (Gen 2:17; 3:6,11). Hence Paul could write generically, "Where there is no law, there is no transgression" (Rom 4:15). "Apart from the law Sin lies dead; I was once alive apart from the law, but when the commandment came, Sin revived, and I died" (Rom 7:8b-9a). So Paul depicts humanity first in the law-less period and then in the period of *Tôrāh.*

(3) The law also laid a curse on the human beings under its authority. Paul derived this idea from Deut 27:26, quoted in Gal 3:10: "Cursed be everyone who abides not by all the things written in the book of the law and does them not!" In this way the law brought *Anthrōpos* "under condemnation" (Rom 8:1), because it was really a "dispensation of death" (2 Cor 3:7), a "dispensation of condemnation" (3:9). To formulate the anomaly pointedly, Paul exclaims, "Did that which is good, then, bring death to me?" (Rom 7:13). Did the God-given *Nomos* bring humanity into the clutches of *Thanatos?* Paul's answer: "Yes," and it so happened that the true colors of *Hamartia*

might be shown up, "that sin might be shown to be sin" (Rom 7:13). All of this reveals the anomalous situation that *Anthrōpos* is in as a result of the law. But how could this be?

95 Paul has two different explanations: one in Gal, and one in Romans—a difference that is not always duly noted.

(1) In Gal, Paul sets forth an extrinsic explanation, ascribing to the law of Moses a temporary role in salvation history: "Now before faith came, we were held in custody under the law, imprisoned until faith was to be revealed; so the law was our custodian [*paidagōgos*] until Christ came that we might be justified by faith" (Gal 3:23–24). *Nomos* is depicted as the slave who in the Hellenistic world kept the school-age boy in tow, conducted him to and from classes, and supervised his study and conduct. The law thus disciplined humanity until the coming of Christ, during the period of *Anthrōpos'* minority. This provisional role of the law is also seen in its being added 430 years after the promises made to Abraham (3:17). Paul's chronology may be off by several centuries, but his point is that the law appeared on the stage *later,* and its inferiority to the promises is also manifest in that it was promulgated by angels (3:19; cf. Deut 33:2 LXX) and through a mediator (3:20, Moses). This temporary role of the law and its inferior status in salvation history did not nullify the "covenant previously ratified by God so as to make the promise void" (3:18).

(2) When Paul came to write Rom, he probably realized that the explanation of the anomaly set forth in Gal was not very satisfactory, not coming to grips with *Anthrōpos'* inability to observe the God-given law. In composing Rom 7:13–8:4, then, Paul abandoned the extrinsic explanation and used a more intrinsic one, that is, a philosophical explanation of the human predicament. In Rom he shows that the difficulty is not with the law, but with humanity in its this-worldly condition of *sarx,* "flesh," alienated from God and hostile to him. Because of this condition, *Anthrōpos* or *Egō* is weak and dominated by indwelling *Hamartia:* "I am carnal (*sarkinos*), sold under Sin" (7:14). The evil force, *Hamartia,* introduced into the world of human existence by Adam's transgression, has kept *Anthrōpos* in bondage because he is basically "carnal." Though he recognizes God's law with his "mind," he recognizes another principle at work in him that is at war with it: "It is no longer I that do it, but Sin that dwells in me" (7:17). Though the *Egō* "serves the law of God with the mind, it serves the law of Sin with the flesh" (7:25); that is, the human mind acknowledges God's law for what it is, but its weak human condition as flesh is in bondage to Sin, which Paul even figuratively calls *nomos,* "the law of sin," an appositional genitive.

96 Paul has a solution for this anomaly created by the Mosaic law in human existence. For the observance of it, Paul substituted faith in Christ Jesus, "who was handed over for our trespasses and raised up for our justification" (Rom 4:25). Yet once again his solution is proposed in two ways.

(1) In Gal, Paul emphasizes that in the third period of salvation history *Anthrōpos* has come of age and reached his majority; he is no longer under the custodian, no longer "under guardians and trustees" and awaiting "the date set by the father" (Gal 4:2). That date has been reached; "in the fulness of time" Christ Jesus was sent by the Father to ransom us from bondage and free us from the law. As a result, the believer is no longer a school-age boy in tow, but a son in the full sense, who cries out "Abba, Father" and has become the heir of the promises made to Abraham, who himself found uprightness in God's sight, not by observing the law, but by faith (Gal 3:16–22; 4:3–6; cf. Gen 15:16). To be noted again is the temporal aspect of the solution that Paul presents in Gal; it corresponds to the temporal, extrinsic explanation of the anomaly. True, Paul does introduce an intrinsic element into Gal when he speaks of the Spirit "sent into our hearts" (4:6), enabling us to cry "Abba, Father" and revealing our adoptive sonship. But even that adoption is still only in terms of a new stage in salvation history.

(2) In Rom, the solution is proposed in terms of the intrinsic anomaly itself. In Rom 7:24 Paul exclaims, "Wretched being that I am, who will rescue me from this doomed body?" His answer: "Thanks be to God, [it is done] through Jesus Christ our Lord!" His answer is further explained in Rom 8:1–4, "Now, then, there is no condemnation for those who are in Christ Jesus, for the law of the Spirit of life in Christ Jesus has freed me from the law of sin and death. For God has done what the law, weakened by the flesh, could not do; he sent his own Son in the likeness of sinful flesh and because of sin; he has condemned sin in the flesh in order that the just requirement of the law might be achieved in us who walk not according to the flesh, but according to the Spirit." Here the solution to the anomaly is not sought in terms of salvation history or the temporal character of the law. Rather, "God's love has been poured into our hearts through the holy Spirit that has been given to us" (5:5). This "Spirit of life in Christ Jesus" (8:2) brings it about that *Anthrōpos* now stands before God's tribunal as "justified," i.e., acquitted, through the cross and resurrection of Christ Jesus. Thus a human being achieves the status before God that the observance of the law of Moses was supposed to achieve. What the law could not achieve (8:3), God himself has brought about in Christ Jesus.

97 Such a solution of the anomaly of the law in human existence has to cope with the highly contested verse in Rom 10:4, where Paul speaks of Christ as *telos nomou*, the "end of the law." That expression might seem to allude to the "end" of the period of the *Tôrāh*. But *telos* can mean either "end, termination" or "goal, purpose, *finis*." In the former sense, Christ would be the end of the law as the termination of all human striving to achieve uprightness in God's sight through the observance of the law. Whereas this sense might fit the temporal perspective of Gal, is it suitable for Rom? Unfortunately, the second sense of the phrase as a final or purposive expression has often been related to the "custodian" of Gal 3:24, understood as a teacher who trained the schoolboy for life. The law would have been schooling humanity for Christ. But the ancient *paidagōgos* was not a pedagogue or teacher in our modern sense, nor does *eis Christon* (Gal 3:24) have a final sense; it is temporal (see E. Käsemann, *Commentary on Romans* [GR, 1980] 282). Ultimately, however, the final sense of *telos nomou* is preferable because of the Rom context; it is logically related to the metaphor of the chase or race in Rom 9:31–33: "Gentiles who were not pursuing uprightness" actually achieved it [through faith in Christ Jesus], whereas "Israel that was pursuing the law of uprightness" did not "attain [that] law." This metaphor clearly involves a goal, and in v. 32 Paul explains the reason of Israel's failure: It did not pursue that goal "through faith, but as if [it were based] on works," and so it tripped over the Isaian stumbling block (Isa 28:16; 18:14–15). Though Paul commends Israel's "zeal for God" (Rom 10:2), misconceived through it was, he depicts Israel "seeking to set up its own uprightness," instead of submitting to "the uprightness of God," that is, to a process that begins in God who is himself *ṣaddîq* (Jer 12:1; Ps 11:7), or possibly even an "uprightness from God that depends on faith" (Phil 3:9). Such a pursuit implies a goal; hence the preference for *telos* as "goal" in Rom 10:4. What Israel sought to attain has now been achieved through faith in Christ. Even Rom 3:21, "apart from [the observance of] the law" (*chōris nomou*) does not militate against this interpretation, because what was the goal of the law (uprightness in God's sight) is achieved through Christ, and not by mere observance of the law. Similarly, Rom 8:2–3 does not demand the translation of *telos* as "termination," for Rom 8:4 makes it clear that "the just requirement of the law is fulfilled in us who walk not according to the flesh, but according to the Spirit." In other words, through grace and faith in Christ, God has brought it about that humanity fulfills what the law requires.

98   There is, however, yet another aspect of the law that is the key to the fuller understanding of Christ as the goal of the law in Rom. In Gal 5:6, Paul speaks of the sole validity of *pistis di' agapēs energoumenē*, "faith working itself out through love." He never explains this phrase in Gal, but one can find an explanation in Rom 13:8–10, where he speaks of the Mosaic law and strikingly regards love not only as something owed to others, but even as "the fulfillment of the law." Even if one were to insist that "fulfillment" is not necessarily the same as *telos*, the final sense of the latter term becomes clear when Paul says, "Love does no wrong to a neighbor; hence love is the fulfillment of the law." Faith in the Christian sense, introduced into human history by the death and resurrection of Christ Jesus, when it works itself out through love, is understood by Paul as accomplishing what the law was intended to accomplish. Only Paul has such a christological understanding of the law of Moses among NT writers.

99   With such an understanding of the law, Paul can even say, "I through the law died to the law that I might live for God" (Gal 2:19). Paul thinks of the

Christian as co-crucified with Christ, and what Christ accomplished through his death and resurrection is something in which Christians share so that they now live for God. But how has this been accomplished by a death to the law through the law? In Gal 3, Paul explains how the curse that was levelled on those who had to live under the law has been removed by Christ who "redeemed us from the curse of the law, by becoming a curse for us" (3:13). Here one cannot make use of Aristotelian logic, for Paul's argument depends on two different senses of the term "curse." In v. 10 the "curse" meant is that of Deut 27:26, whereas the "curse" in v. 13 is rather that of Deut 21:23, "Cursed be everyone who hangs upon a tree," a curse formulated against the dead body of an executed criminal hanged from a tree as a deterrent to further crime: The body was not to be allowed to hang beyond sundown, lest it defile the land. In late pre-Christian Palestinian Judaism that curse was applied to crucified persons; their dead bodies were not to be permitted to hang overnight (see J. A. Fitzmyer, *TAG*, 125–46). Such a curse was pronounced over the crucified body of Jesus; and by becoming a "curse" in that sense, Paul argues, Christ removed the "curse" of the law (Deut 27:26) from those who were under it. This does not mean, however, that the relation of human beings to God is completely removed from the realm of law, but that that relation, though still judicial and forensic, finds another mode of achievement or fulfillment than through the "deeds of the law." In this way Rom 7:4,6 are to be understood.

100 A final comment. Paul often uses the expression *erga nomou*, "deeds/ works of the law," that is, deeds prescribed by the Mosaic law (Gal 2:16; 3:2,5,10; Rom 2:15; 3:20,27,28). One even gets the impression that this phrase was a sort of slogan current in Paul's day. Yet it is never found as such either in the OT or in later rabbinic literature (see *TDNT* 2, 646; Str-B 3, 160–62). It is used, however, in QL (*ma ͨ ăśê tôrāh*, "deeds of the law," 4QFlor [=4Q174] 1–2 i 7; cf. 1QS 6:18; 1QpHab 7:11). At times Paul shortens the phrase and uses merely *erga*, "deeds" (Rom 4:2,6; 9:11,32; 11:6). From this shortening stems the difficulty that his slogan later encountered, when his teaching about justification by grace through faith, apart from works, was being heard in a different Christian context. Recall the correction (not of his teaching, but of a caricature of it) that is found in Jas 2:14–26; see J. Reumann, "*Righteousness*" (→ 70 above) § 270–75, 413.

(Benoit, P., "The Law and the Cross according to St Paul: Romans 7:7–8:4," *Jesus and the Gospel: Volume 2* [London, 1974] 11–39. Bruce, F. F., "Paul and the Law of Moses," *BJRL* 57 [1974–75] 259–79. Cranfield, C. E. B., "St. Paul and the Law," *SJT* 17 [1964] 43–68. Dülmen, A. von, *Die Theologie des Gesetzes bei Paulus* [SBM 5; Stuttgart, 1968]. Fitzmyer, J. A., "Paul and the Law," *TAG*, 186–201. Gundry, R. H., "Grace, Works, and Staying Saved in Paul," *Bib* 66 [1985] 1–38. Hahn, F., "Das Gesetzesverständnis im Römerbrief und Galaterbrief," *ZNW* 67 [1976] 29–63. Hübner, H., *Law in Paul's Thought* [Edinburgh, 1984]. Lang, F., "Gesetz und Bund bei Paulus," *Recht*, 305–20. Larsson, E.,

"Paul: Law and Salvation," *NTS* 31 [1985] 425–36. Räisänen, H., *Paul and the Law* [WUNT 29: Tübingen, 1983]. Sanders, E. P., *Paul, the Law, and the Jewish People* [Phl, 1983]. Schäfer, P., "Die Torah der messianischen Zeit," *ZNW* 65 [1974] 27–42. Wilckens, U., "Zur Entwicklung des paulinischen Gesetzesverständnisses," *NTS* 28 [1982] 154–90.)

101 (c) HUMAN BEINGS. Part of Paul's picture of humanity before Christ's coming is the makeup of a human being (*anthrōpos*). Inability to observe the Mosaic law stems in part from the carnal condition of a human being as *sarkinos*. What does Paul mean by this? To explain, we must try to ascertain what he means by *sōma*, "body," *sarx*, "flesh," *psychē*, "soul," *pneuma*, "spirit," *nous*, "mind," and *kardia*, "heart." Paul does not describe a human being *in se*; rather, he hints at different relations of humanity vis-à-vis God and the world in which the person lives. These terms, then, do not designate parts of a human being but rather aspects of the person as seen from different perspectives.

102 A popular, common conception of the human being as made up of two elements is found at times in Paul's writings (1 Cor 5:3; 7:34; 2 Cor 12:2-3). The visible, tangible, biological part made up of members is called *sōma*, "body" (Rom 12:4; 1 Cor 12:14–26). Though Paul seems at times to mean by it only the flesh, blood, and bones (Gal 1:16; 1 Cor 13:3; 2 Cor 4:10; 10:10; Rom 1:24), he normally means far more. A human being does not merely have a *sōma*; one is *sōma*. It is a way of saying "self" (Phil 1:20; Rom 6:12–13; cf. 1 Cor 6:15 and 12:27). It denotes a human being as a whole, complex, living organism, even as a person, especially when he or she is the subject to whom something happens or is the object of one's own action (1 Cor 9:27; Rom 6:12–13; 8:13; 12:1; cf. R. Bultmann, *TNT* 1, 195). A corpse is not a *sōma*, but there is no form of human existence for Paul without a body in this full sense (see Phil 3:21; 1 Cor 15:35–45; but cf. 2 Cor 5:2–4; 12:2–3; 5:6–8). When Paul uses *sōma* in a pejorative sense, speaking of its "desires or passions" (Rom 6:12; 8:13), of the "body of sin" (Rom 6:6), of the "body of humiliation" (Phil 3:21), or of "the body of death" (Rom 8:3), he really means the human being under the sway of some power like sin (Rom 7:14,18,23; 8:13). In these cases, the "body" is the sin-ruled self (Rom 7:23), the human condition before the coming of Christ—or even after that coming for those who do not live in Christ.

103 In the OT the word *bāśār* expresses the idea of both "body" and "flesh." Paul reflects this OT notion when he uses *sarx* as a synonym for *sōma* (1 Cor 6:16, quoting Gen 2:24; 2 Cor 4:10–11; cf. Gal 4:13; 6:17). In these cases "flesh" means the physical body. The phrase "flesh and blood" denotes a human being (Gal 1:16; 1 Cor 15:50), connoting natural frailty. It is a late OT expression (Sir 14:18; 17:31). But *sarx* alone can denote whole human being, human nature (Rom 6:19). However, the more typically Pauline use of the word flesh connotes natural, material, and visible human existence, weak and earthbound, the human creature left to itself: "No flesh can boast of anything before God" (1 Cor 1:29). "People controlled by the flesh think of what pertains to the flesh" (Rom 8:5); they cannot please God (Rom 8:8). The "deeds of the flesh" are set forth in Gal 5:19–21; and it should be superfluous to note that for Paul, "flesh" is not restricted to the area of sex. He identifies the *egō* and *sarx* and finds no good in them (Rom 7:18). This notion is prominent in the Pauline contrast of "flesh" and "Spirit," which compares a human being subject to earthly tendencies with a human being under the influence of God's Spirit (Gal 3:3; 4:29; Rom 8:4–9,13).

104 Similarly, *psychē* is not just the vital principle of biological activity, but as in the OT, it denotes a "living being, living person" (Hebr *nepeš;* 1 Cor 15:45). It expresses the vitality, consciousness, intelligence, and volition of a human being (1 Thess 2:8; Phil 2:30; 2 Cor 12:15; Rom 11:3; 16:4). Even when it seems to mean nothing more than "self" (2 Cor 1:23; Rom 2:9; 13:1), it connotes the conscious, purposeful vitality of the self. Still it is only the earthly, natural aspect of a living human being. Normally, Paul does not use *psychē* in a derogatory sense; but it is clearly the life of *sarx*, not the life dominated by the Spirit. Hence he calls the one who lives without the Spirit of God *psychikos*, "material" (1 Cor 2:14), not "spiritual" (*pneumatikos*).

105 In 1 Thess 5:23, Paul lines up a threesome, *sōma, psychē,* and *pneuma.* In this case, *pneuma* does not designate the holy Spirit (cf. Rom 8:16; 1 Cor 2:10–11). Joined to *sōma* and *psychē*, which denote the whole human being under different aspects, *pneuma* would seem to be yet another aspect. But it is not always easy to distinguish *pneuma* in this sense from *psychē* (cf. Phil 1:27; 2 Cor 12:18). If anything, *pneuma* suggests the knowing and willing self and, as such, the aspect that is particularly apt to receive the Spirit of God. Sometimes, however, it is a mere substitute for the personal pronoun (Gal 6:18; 2 Cor 2:13; 7:13; Rom 1:9; Phlm 25).

106 *Nous,* "mind," for Paul seems to describe a human being as a knowing and judging subject; it designates a capacity for intelligent understanding, planning, and decision (cf. 1 Cor 1:10; 2:16; Rom 14:5). In Rom 7:23 it is the understanding self that hears God's will addressed to it in the law, agrees with God's will, and accepts it as its own. It is the capacity to recognize what can be known about God from his creation (Rom 1:20); the *nooumena* are the things that the *nous* can grasp. There is really little difference in Paul's use of *nous* and *kardia*, "heart," which, as in the OT, often means "mind." If anything, *kardia* would connote the more responsive and emotional reactions of the intelligent, planning self. For it "loves" (2 Cor 7:3; 8:16), "grieves" (Rom 9:2), "plans" (1 Cor 4:5), "lusts" (Rom 1:24), and "suffers" (2 Cor 2:4). It doubts and believes (Rom 10:6–10), is hardened (2 Cor 3:14), and is impenitent (Rom 2:5); but it can be strengthened (1 Thess 3:13; Gal 4:6; 2 Cor 1:22). For the relation of "mind" and "conscience," →144 below.

107 All these aspects of human existence are summed up in *zōē*, "life," a gift of God that expresses the concrete existence of a human being as the subject of his or her actions. Yet life before the coming of Christ is one lived "according to the flesh" (Rom 8:12; cf. Gal 2:20). With all the capacities for conscious, intelligent, and purposeful planning of one's life, a human being without Christ remains one who has not been able to achieve the destined goal. Of this situation, Paul can only say, "All have sinned and fall short of the glory of God" (Rom 3:23), the latter being for him Christian destiny (cf. Rom 8:18–23). This sketch of the human condition before the coming of Christ has at times hinted at the difference that Christ's coming has made for humanity; a fuller description of that difference now follows.

(Gundry, R. H., *Sōma in Biblical Theology with Emphasis on Pauline Anthropology* [SNTSMS 29; Cambridge, U.K., 1976]. Jewett, R., *Paul's Anthropological Terms* [AGJU 10; Leiden, 1971]. Kümmel, W. G., *Man in the New Testament* [rev. ed.; London, 1963]. Robinson, J. A. T., *The Body: A Study in Pauline Theology* [SBT 5; London, 1952]. Sand, A., *Der Begriff "Fleisch" in den paulinischen Hauptbriefen* [BU 2; Regensburg, 1967]. Stacey, W. D., *The Pauline View of Man in Relation to Its Judaic and Hellenistic Background* [London, 1956].)

108 (B) Humanity in Christ. Christ's salvific activity has brought about a new union of humanity with God. Paul calls it a "new creation" (→ 79 above), for it has introduced a new mode of existence into human history in which Christ and the Christian enjoy, as it were, a symbiosis. Human beings share in this new life by faith and baptism, which incorporate the person into Christ and his church; this incorporation finds a unique expression in the eucharist. To such elements of Pauline theology, often regarded as aspects of the subjective redemption, we now turn.

109 (a) FAITH AND LOVE. The experience whereby a human being begins to apprehend the effects of the Christ-event is for Paul *pistis*, "faith." This experience is a reaction to the gospel, to the "preached word" (Rom 10:8). Paul's most elaborate treatment is found in Rom 10, a chapter that must be studied in detail. The experience begins with a "hearing" (*akoē*, 10:17) of the gospel or of the "word" about Christ and his salvific role. This hearing results in an assent of the mind that acknowledges that "Jesus is Lord" in one's existence (10:9). It ends, however, as *hypakoē pisteōs*, usually translated as the "obedience of faith" (1:5; 16:26), but which really means "a hearing-under" and connotes for Paul the "submission" or the "commitment" of the whole person to God in Christ. "If with your lips you acknowledge that Jesus is Lord and with your heart you believe that God raised him from the dead, you will be saved" (10:9). Thus the faith that one is asked to put in God or Christ (1 Thess 4:14; 1 Cor 1:21–23; Rom 4:24) is not a mere intellectual assent to the proposition that "Jesus is Lord." It is a vital, personal commitment, engaging the whole person to Christ in all his or her relations with God, other human beings, and the world. It is thus an awareness of the difference the lordship of Christ has made in human history. This awareness underlies the statement of Paul, "It is no longer I who live, but Christ who lives in me; and even now the physical life I am living [lit., what I now live in the flesh] I live through faith in the Son of God who loved me and gave himself for me" (Gal 2:20). Such a faith far transcends the OT idea of fidelity. As *hypakoē*, it is full acceptance of Christian dedication (Rom 6:16–17; 16:19), to the exclusion of all reliance on self, or on what Paul calls "boasting" (Rom 3:27). The basis of this experience is a new union with God in Christ, an ontological reality that is not immediately perceived by human consciousness but must be allowed to pervade the psychological level of existence so that one's conscious activity is guided by it. This is the integrated Christian life that Paul envisages (see Gal 2:20; 2 Cor 10:5).

110 Such faith is a gift of God, just as is the whole salvific process (Rom 3:24–25; 6:14; 11:6; 12:3). This is the underlying notion in the whole discussion of Abraham's faith in Rom 4. (In the Deutero-Pauline passage of Eph 2:8 this idea becomes explicit: "It is by his [Christ's] favor that you have been saved through faith; and this does not come from you; it is the gift of God.") But because God accosts a human being as a responsible person, that person can accept or reject God's gracious call. Faith is thus only the acceptance or the response on the part of the human being who realizes that the initiative rests with God. The one who does not respond is regarded by Paul as disobedient and committed to "the god of this age" (2 Cor 4:4), hence, culpable and "perishing."

111 In the polemical contexts in which Paul rejects the "deeds of the law" as a means to justification, he stresses that this justification comes through "faith" (Gal 2:16; Rom 3:28; cf. Phil 3:9). However, the full sense of that faith demands that the Christian manifest it in conduct through deeds of love. "In union with Christ Jesus neither circumcision nor the lack of it means anything, but only faith working itself out through love" (Gal 5:6). This is why Paul continually exhorts his Christian converts to the practice of all sorts of good deeds, why he includes a hortatory section in almost every one of his letters. Christian faith is not only a freedom from the law, from sin, and from the *sarx*-self, but also a freedom to serve others in love or charity (Gal 5:13). For Paul, love (*agapē*) is an openness, an outgoing concern and respect of one person for another/others in concrete acts that result in the diminution of the lover's "self." See Phlm 9–12; Gal 5:13; Rom 12:9–13. It is a way of

Christian life that is extraordinary (*kath' hyberbolēn*, 1 Cor 12:31), surpassing even all the charismatic manifestations of the Spirit. Interpreters may debate about the character of 1 Cor 13, whether it is hymnic or a rhetorical description, but one finds there Paul's praise of love in Christian life: its indispensability, its eleven characteristics (positive and negative), and its perdurance and superiority. But love is also for Paul the summation of the law (Rom 13:8–10; Gal 5:14). In other words, the person motivated by a faith that works itself out through love is not in reality concerned about "the deeds of the law," but finds himself or herself doing all that the law has required. In this way faith for Paul turns out to be more than a mere assent to monotheism (cf. Jas 2:14–26). The root of such love is the Spirit (Gal 5:22) and ultimately the love of the Father, for the "love of God" is poured out into our hearts (Rom 5:5; 8:28), and thus it is just as much a grace of God as faith itself. Such service of others is not accomplished without the activity of God in human beings: "God is at work in you both to will and to work for his good pleasure" (Phil 2:13). This is why Paul formulates the hymn to the love of God made manifest in Christ Jesus (Rom 8:31–39), and speaks of the controlling love of Christ in Christian life (2 Cor 5:14).

(Barth, G., "*Pistis*, etc." *EWNT* 3, 216–31. Binder, H., *Der Glaube bei Paulus* [Berlin, 1968]. Bultmann, R. and A. Weiser, "*Pisteuō*, etc.," *TDNT* 6, 174–228. Daalen, D. H. van, " 'Faith' according to Paul," *ExpTim* 87 [1975–76] 83–85. Kuss, O., "Der Glaube nach den paulinischen Hauptbriefen," *Auslegung und Verkündigung I* [Regensburg, 1963] 187–212. Lohse, E., "Emuna und Pistis," *ZNW* 68 [1977] 147–63. Lührmann, D., *Glaube im frühen Christentum* [Gütersloh, 1976]. Michel, O., "Faith," *NIDNTT* 1, 587–606. Walter, N., "Christus-glaube und heidnische Religiosität in paulinischen Gemeinden," *NTS* 25 [1978–79] 422–42.

Bornkamm, G., *Early Christian Experience* [NY, 1969] 180–93. Descamps, A., "La charité, résumé de la loi," *RDTour* 8 [1953] 123–29; "L'Hymne à la charité (I *Cor.*, XIII), " ibid. 241–45. Furnish, V. P., *The Love Command in the New Testament* [Nash, 1972] 91–131. Lyonnet, S., "Foi et charité d'après Saint Paul," *Foi et salut selon Saint Paul (Epître aux Romains 1,16)* [AnBib 42; Rome, 1970] 211–31. Navone, J. J., "Love in the Message of Paul," *Worship* 40 [1966] 437–44. Perkins, P., *Love Commands in the New Testament* [NY, 1982]. Sanders, J. T., "First Corinthians 13: Its Interpretation since the First World War," *Int* 20 [1966] 159–87. Spicq, C., *Agape in the New Testament* [3 vols.; St. Louis, 1963–66] 2, 1–341. Wischmeyer, O., "Traditionsgeschichtliche Untersuchung der paulinischen Aussagen über die Liebe," *ZNW* 74 [1983] 222–36.)

112 (b) BAPTISM. Paul's stress on the role of faith in the human response to the Christ-event is, however, adequately understood only when it is linked to his teaching on baptism. This initiatory rite, which incorporates human beings into Christ and the church, already existed in pre-Pauline Christianity, but it is Paul who developed its significance. The formulas he uses (Rom 10:9;

1 Cor 12:3) possibly echo primitive baptismal creeds; yet it is Paul who teaches that the condition of Christians as "sons of God through faith" is owing to their baptism "into Christ" (Gal 3:26–27). Christians so washed have been "sanctified and made upright" (1 Cor 6:11). They have "put on Christ," as if they were putting on a new garment (an allusion to the robe worn in the baptismal ceremony?). (In Eph 5:26 a disciple of Paul may allude to the rite itself, in speaking of a "washing of water" and a "word" [= formula?].)

113 Through baptism the Christian is actually identified with the death, burial, and resurrection of Christ. The early church preserved a recollection that Jesus referred to his own death as a "baptism" (Mark 10:38; Luke 12:50). But Paul's view of the effects of the Christ-event led him to identify, as it were, Christians with the very phases of Christ's salvific activity; "one died for all, therefore all died" (2 Cor 5:14). Prima facie, this may seem like a mere assertion of the vicarious nature of Christ's death, but it must be understood in the light of the following: "Through baptism we have been buried with him in death, so that just as Christ was raised from the dead through the Father's glory, so we too might live a new life. For if we have grown into union with him by undergoing a death like his, so we shall do by being raised to life like him" (Rom 6:4–5). Paul's comparison of baptism with the death, burial, and resurrection of Christ is often thought to allude to the rite of immersion. Though this mode of baptism may be difficult to certify for the first century AD, Paul's symbolism is sufficiently preserved if the baptized person is thought of as somehow under the water. Identified with Christ in death, the Christian dies to the law and to sin (Gal 2:19; Rom 6:6,10; 7:4). Identified with Christ in his resurrection, one shares a new life and the very vitality of the risen Christ and his Spirit (1 Cor 6:17). The Christian "has grown together" with Christ through this likeness of his death, burial, and resurrection (Rom 6:5). The one who dies in baptism becomes a "new creation" (Gal 6:15; 2 Cor 5:17). (The Deutero-Paulines will express it in terms of the Christian already enjoying a new "heavenly" existence [Col 2:12–13]. "Though we were dead because of our offenses, God has made us live again with Christ. By his grace we are saved, and he has raised us up with Christ Jesus and made us sit down with him in the heavenly realm" [Eph 2:5–6].)

114 This is no mere individualistic experience for Christians, but a corporate one, for through baptism a special union of Christians is formed. "We have all, Jews or Greeks, slaves or free men, been baptized in one spirit to form one body" (1 Cor 12:13; cf. Gal 3:28). Human beings, therefore, attain salvation by identification with a salvific community (*Heilsgemeinde*), by incorporation into the "body of Christ." This is why Paul compares baptism to Israel's passage through the waters of the Reed Sea (1 Cor. 10:1–2); in the waters of baptism the new "Israel of God" (Gal 6:16) is formed.

115 Paul never quotes a primitive baptismal formula such as Matt 28:19; yet he seems to echo an early Trinitarian theologoumenon on baptism: "You have been washed, sanctified, and made upright in the name of the Lord Jesus Christ and in the Spirit of our God" (1 Cor 6:11). The baptized Christian becomes a "temple of the holy Spirit" (1 Cor 6:19), an adopted child of the Father in virtue of the communication of the Spirit (Gal 4:6; Rom 8:9,14–17). The Spirit so received is the constitutive principle of filial adoption and the dynamic source of Christian life and conduct. "All who are led by God's Spirit are children of God" (Rom 8:14). Such passages are the basis of the later teaching about the relation of the baptized Christian to the persons of the Trinity. Only indirectly does Paul make use of a baptismal formula, "in the name of" (*eis to onoma tou* . . . , 1 Cor 1:13,15; 6:11). Though it expresses proprietorship and suggests that the baptized person becomes the property of Christ, Paul prefers to speak of the person as baptized "into Christ" (Rom 6:3; Gal 3:27), that is, symbolically plunged into Christ himself.

(Beasley-Murray, G. R., *Baptism in the New Testament* [London, 1962]. Bieder, W., *"Baptizō, etc." EWNT* 1, 459–69. Bornkamm, G., *Early Christian Experience* [NY, 1969] 71–86. Delling, G., *Die Zueignung des Heils in der Taufe* [Berlin, 1961]. Dunn, J. D. G., *Baptism in the Holy Spirit* [Naperville, IL, 1970]. Frankemölle, H., *Das Taufverständnis des Paulus* [SBS 47; Stuttgart, 1970]. Hartman, L., " 'Into the Name of Jesus,' " *NTS* 20 [1973–74] 432–40. Iacono, V., "Il battesimo in S. Paolo," *RivB* 3 [1955] 348–62. Kaye, B. N., *"Baptizein eis* with Special Reference to Romans 6," *SE VI*, 281–86. Kuss, O., "Zur vorpaulinischen Tauflehre im Neuen Testament," *Auslegung und Verkündigung I* [Regensburg, 1963] 98–120; "Zur paulinischen und nachpaulinischen Tauflehre im Neuen Testament," ibid., 121–50. Lampe, G. W. H., *The Seal of the Spirit* [2d ed.; London, 1967]. Schnackenburg, R., *Baptism in the Thought of St. Paul* [Oxford, 1964]. Voss, G., "Glaube und Taufe in den Paulusbriefen," *US* 25 [1970] 371–78.)

116 (c) INCORPORATION INTO CHRIST. To appreciate the effects of faith and baptism as seen by Paul, we turn to his ideas on the intimate union of Christ and Christians, expressed by pregnant prepositional phrases and by the figure of the "body of Christ."

117 (i) *Prepositional Phrases.* Paul uses mainly four prepositions with "Christ" as their object to suggest different facets of Christ's influence on the life of the Christian. The use of each of them is varied and often rich with nuances. We can only indicate here some of the most important implications. The four prepositions are *dia, eis, syn,* and *en.*

118 The prep. *dia,* "through," normally expresses the mediation of Christ in a statement of which the subject is the Father. It may denote the mediation of Christ in some activity of his earthly ministry (1 Thess 5:9), of his present status as Lord (Rom 1:5), or of his eschatological role (1 Thess 4:14). It is a

4/4

phrase that opens up, as it were, the path that leads to the Christian's experience *en Christō*, and eventually *syn Christō*.

119 The prep. *eis*, "into," especially in the phrase *eis Christon*, has at times been taken as an abridgement of *eis to onoma Christou*, "into the name of Christ." With the vb. *baptizein* this is possible (→115 above). But *eis Christon* is also used with *pisteuein*, "believe." In fact, the phrase is mainly found in these two contexts: belief or baptism in Christ. It pregnantly expresses the movement toward Christ that these initial experiences imply, the beginning of the Christian's condition *en Christō* (see 1 Cor 10:2). Torn from one's original condition ("in Adam," 1 Cor 15:22), from one's natural inclinations ("in the flesh," Rom 7:5), and from one's ethnic background ("under the law," 1 Cor 9:20), one is solemnly introduced "into Christ" in faith and baptism. *Eis Christon* denotes, then, the movement of incorporation.

120 The prep. *syn*, "with," is used not only with the object "Christ" but is also compounded with verbs and adjectives and can in these constructions express a double relation of the Christian to Christ. Either it suggests an identification of the Christian with the preeminently salvific acts of the Christ-event, or else it denotes an association of the Christian with Christ in eschatological glory. On the one hand, the identification is seen above all in the compounds of *syn-*. Aside from generic expressions like *symmorphos* "formed with him," *symphytos*, "grown together with him," *synklēronomos*, "heir with him," these words refer to some phase of Christ's existence from his passion and death on: *sympaschein*, "suffer with," *systaurousthai*, "be crucified with," *synapothnēskein*, "die with," *synthaptesthai*, "be buried with," *syndoxazesthai*, "be glorified with," *synzan*, "live with." (In the Deutero-Paulines one also finds *synegeirein*, "raise with.") By contrast, the Christian is never said to be born with Christ, to be baptized with him, or to be tempted with him. Such events of the life of Jesus were not significant for Paul's soteriology (→18 above). On the other hand, *syn Christō* expresses the association of the Christian with Christ in eschatological glory; one is destined to be "with Christ" (1 Thess 4:17 [significantly, *syn Kyriō*]; Rom 6:8; 8:32; 2 Cor 4:14). Hence *syn* pregnantly expresses two poles of the Christian experience, identification with Christ at its beginning, and association with him at its term. In the meantime the Christian is *en Christō*.

121 The prep. *en*, "in," with the object "Christ" occurs 165 times in Paul's letters (including *en Kyriō*, "in the Lord," and *en autō*, "in him"). Ever since the studies of A. Deissmann, the preposition has often been interpreted in a local, spatial sense, and *Christos* has been understood mystically of the glorified Lord identified with the Spirit as some spiritual atmosphere in which Christians are bathed. This is supposed to be Paul's mysticism. But subsequent studies of E. Lohmeyer, A. Schweitzer, F. Büchsel, and others have brought out other aspects of the phrase (metaphysical, eschatological, dynamic, etc.). A detailed summary is impossible here, but several distinctions should be noted. (1) With the object *Kyrios*, the phrase usually occurs in greetings, blessings, exhortations (often with imperatives), and formulations of Paul's apostolic plans and activity. The title *Kyrios* denotes, then, the influence of the risen Lord in practical and ethical areas of Christian conduct. *En Kyriō* hardly ever reflects Jesus' historical, earthly activity or his eschatological function; rather, it implies his present, sovereign dominion in the life of the Christian. Paul tells the Christian to become "in the Lord" what one really is "in Christ." (2) With the object *Christos*, the phrase frequently has an instrumental sense, when it refers to the historical, earthly activity of Jesus (Gal 2:17; 2 Cor 5:19; Rom 3:24; [Col 1:14; Eph 2:10]). In this sense the phrase is often close in meaning to *dia Christou*. (3) The most common use of *en Christō* is to express the close union of Christ and the Christian, an inclusion that connotes a symbiosis of the two. "If anyone is in Christ, one is a new creature" (2 Cor 5:17). This vital union, however, can also be expressed as "Christ in me" (Gal 2:20; 2 Cor 13:5; Rom 8:10; [Col 1:27; Eph 3:17]). The result is that one belongs to Christ (2 Cor 10:7) or is "of Christ"—a "mystical" genitive expressing the same idea (Rom 16:16). The phrase should not be limited to a spatial dimension, for it often connotes a dynamic influence of Christ on the Christian who is incorporated into him. The Christian so incorporated becomes a member of the whole Christ, of the body of Christ. Needless to say, at times one hesitates about the precise nuance (instrumental? inclusive?).

(Bouttier, M., *En Christ* [Paris, 1962]. Büchsel, F., " 'In Christus' bei Paulus," *ZNW* 42 [1949] 141–58. Deissmann, A., *Die neutestamentliche Formel "in Christo Jesu"* [Marburg, 1892]. Dupont, J., *Syn Christo: L'Union avec le Christ suivant Saint Paul* [Bruges, 1952]. Elliger, W., *"Eis," "En," "Syn," EWNT* 1, 965–68, 1093–96; 3, 697–99. Hess, A. J., *"Dia," EWNT* 1, 712–13. Kuss, O., *Der Römerbrief* [Regensburg, 1957–78] 319–81. Lohmeyer, E., *"Syn Christo," Festgabe für Adolf Deissmann* [Tübingen, 1927] 218–57. Neugebauer, F., *In Christus:* En Christo: *Eine Untersuchung zum paulinischen Glaubensverständnis* [Göttingen, 1961]. Schweitzer, A., *The Mysticism of Paul the Apostle* [NY, 1931]. Schweizer, E., "Dying and Rising with Christ," *NTS* 14 [1967–68] 1–14. Wikenhauser, A., *Pauline Mysticism* [NY, 1961].)

122 (ii) *Body of Christ.* Paul uses the expression *sōma Christou*, "body of Christ," in various senses: of his historical, crucified body (Rom 7:4), of his eucharistic body (1 Cor 10:16; cf. 11:27), and of the church (1 Cor 12:27–28; [cf. Col 2:17; Eph 4:12]). In the last sense it is a figurative way of expressing the corporate identity of Christians with Christ. Absent from his early letters (1 Thess, Gal, Phil) it may appear in 1 Cor, in the letter wherein Paul copes with divisive Christian factions. Christ is not divided, he tells them, formulating a teaching about the unity of all believers in Christ. The symbol of unity is the figure of the body with its members. The origin of the figure is disputed (see J. A. T. Robinson, *The Body*, 55–58; R. Bultmann, *TNT* 1, 299; A. E. Hill, "The Temple"). But it is probably derived by Paul from contemporary Hellenistic notions about the state as the body politic. This idea is found as early as Aristotle (*Polit.* 5.2,7 [1302b, 35–36]) and became part of Stoic philosophy (see Cicero, *Or. Philip.* 8.5.15; Seneca, *Ep. mor.* 95.52; Plutarch, *Coriolanus* 6.3–4). In *Moralia* 426A, Plutarch recalls the ideas of the Stoic Chrysippus and asks, "Is there not often in this world of ours a single body [*sōma hen*] composed of disparate bodies, such as an assembly [*ekklēsia*] or an army or a chorus, each one of which happens to have a faculty of living, thinking, and learning . . . ?" (The collocation of *sōma* and *ekklēsia* here is important.) In this case the philosophical figure expresses the moral unity of members (citizens, soldiers) conspiring together to achieve a common goal (e.g., peace, prosperity, and well-being). In 1 Cor 12:12–27 the figure as used by Paul scarcely transcends this idea of a moral union of the members: The spiritual gifts enjoyed by the Corinthians (wisdom, faith, healing, prophecy, tongues, etc.) are to be used "for the common good" (12:7), not for its disruption. As all the members and limbs of the body conspire for its well-being, so it is with the body of Christ. The usage is similar in the hortatory context of Rom 12:4–5.

123 But more is suggested elsewhere by Paul. In 1 Cor 6:15 he warns against the defilement of the human body by sexual license: "Don't you know that your bodies are members of Christ? Am I to take away the members of Christ and make them members of a harlot? No indeed! Or don't you know that a man who has to do with a harlot makes one body with her? For 'the two,' Scripture says, 'shall become one flesh.'" The union implied here is more than moral; somehow Christ and the Christian share in a union that connotes "one flesh." Recall what was said above (→102–3) about the meaning of *sōma* and *sarx* as designations, not of the physical body as something distinct from the soul, but as equivalents of the whole person under different aspects. In speaking of the "body of Christ" Paul is not speaking merely of members of a society governed by a common objective, but of members of Christ himself; their union is not only corporate but also somehow corporal. A similar conclusion is suggested by 1 Cor 10:16–17, where Paul insists on the union of all Christians achieved by their share in the one eucharistic bread and cup: "Because there is one loaf, we, many as we are, are one body, for we all share the one loaf." The unity of Christians is thus derived from their physical consumption of the one loaf; the oneness implied transcends a mere extrinsic union effected by cooperation to attain a common goal. (The figure of marriage in Eph 5:22–33 also points to the same transcendent union.)

124 And yet Christians and Christ are not physically united like the yolk and the albumen of an egg. Hence theologians later called the union "mystical," an adjective that Paul does not use. The ontological reality that is the basis of the union is the possession of the Spirit of Christ: "We have all been baptized in one Spirit to form one body" (1 Cor 12:13; cf. Rom 8:9–11). The possession of this Spirit springs from the incorporation of believers through faith and baptism; it is, as it were, the term of Paul's christocentric soteriology.

125 However, Paul rarely speaks in 1 Cor and Rom explicitly of the church as the body of Christ; the closest one comes to this identification is 1 Cor 12:27–28. (In the Deutero-Paulines, when the cosmic significance of Christ has dawned, a disciple of Paul links the themes of body and church, which have often appeared separately in the uncontested letters. Now the church is explicitly identified as the body of Christ in various formulations: "He [Christ] is the head of the body, the church" [Col 1:18; cf. 1:24]; God "made him the supreme head of the church, which is his body" [Eph 1:23]. In Eph there is great emphasis on the unity of the church: Christ has broken down the barrier between Jew and Greek; all now share one salvation, for he has "reconciled both in one body to God through the cross" [2:16]. "There is only one body and one Spirit, just as there is only one hope in the calling you have received: one Lord, one faith, one baptism, one God and Father of us all" [4:4]. And yet with all this stress on unity and the oneness of Christians in Christ, there is no mention of *mia ekklēsia*, "one church." Is this just fortuitous? Part of the answer appears below in the discussion of "church" [→133–37]. In the Pastoral Letters, otherwise so preoccupied with church interests, the "body of Christ" makes no appearance.

126 Intimately related to the body theme in the Deutero-Paulines is that of the head: Christ is "the head of the body, the church" [Col 1:18; cf. Eph 1:23]. It may seem that this is a mere extension of the body theme: Having portrayed the union of Christ and Christians by the analogy of the body and its parts, the disciple of Paul would have concluded that Christ must be its head because the head is the most important part of the body, as can be illustrated in contemporary Hellenistic medical writers [see P. Benoit, "Body," 73]. But Paul himself had used the head theme independently of the body theme in his uncontested letters, not as a figure of unity, but as one of subordination. In 1 Cor 11:3–9, Paul argues that women should wear a head-covering in liturgical assemblies because, among other reasons, the order of creation in Gen seems to call for the subordination of woman to husband and the head-covering would be a sign of this status: "Christ is the head of every man, while a woman's head is her husband, and Christ's head is God" [11:3]. Paul plays on two senses of "head": the physical head, which must be covered, and the figurative head, like "head" of a department. In 1 Cor 11, however, there is no mention of "body." There is another instance of this sense of "head" in Col 2:10, where Christ is said to be "the head of every principality and power." In the Deutero-Paulines the body theme and head theme are joined in the picture of the church; and the analogy is exploited with details drawn from contemporary medical teaching: "Let us rather hold to the truth with love; thus we shall fully grow up into union with him who is head, Christ. For in dependence on him the whole body is bonded and knit together" [Eph 4:15–16]. Another aspect of this subordination of Christians to Christ underlies the comparison of Christian marriage and the church: "Just as the church is in subjection to Christ, so too should wives be subject to their husbands" [Eph 5:24].

127 The Christian experience, then, rooted in the historical reality of the physical body of Christ, becomes a living, dynamic union with the individual *risen body* of the *Kyrios*. The corporate union of all Christians must grow to fill out the whole Christ, the *plērōma* of the cosmic Christ [Eph 1:23]. In the lives of individual Christians this means apostolic suffering that fills up what was lacking in Christ's tribulations on behalf of the church [Col 1:24]. This does not mean that apostolic suffering adds anything to the redemptive value of the cross; rather, such suffering on behalf of the church continues in time that which Christ began, but did not finish in time. It must continue until the cosmic dimensions of the church are achieved.)

(Benoit, P., "Body, Head and *Pleroma* in the Epistles of the Captivity," *Jesus and the Gospel, Volume 2* [London, 1974] 51–92. Daines, B., "Paul's Use of the Analogy of the Body of Christ," *EvQ* 50 [1978] 71–78. Harrington, D. J., *God's People in Christ* [Phl, 1980]. Havet, J., "La doctrine paulinienne du 'Corps du Christ,'" *Littérature et théologie pauliniennes* [ed. A. Descamps; RechBib 5; Bruges, 1960] 185–216. Hegermann, H., "Zur Ableitung der Leib-Christi-Vorstellung," *TLZ* 85 [1960] 839–42. Hill, A. E., "The Temple of Asclepius: An Alternate Source for Paul's Body Theology," *JBL* 99 [1980] 437–39. Käsemann, E., "The Theological Problem Presented by the Motif of the Body of Christ," *Perspectives*, 102–21. Meeks, W. A., "In One Body," *God's Christ and His People* [Fest. N. A. Dahl; ed. J. Jervell and W. A. Meeks; Oslo, 1977] 209–21. Ramaroson, L., "L'Eglise, corps du Christ' dans les écrits pauliniens: Simples esquisses," *ScEs* 30 [1978] 129–41. Robinson, J. A. T., *The Body: A Study in Pauline Theology* [SBT 5; London, 1952]. Schweizer, E., "*Sōma*," *EWNT* 3,770–79. Weiss, H.-F., " 'Volk Gottes' und 'Leib Christi': Überlegungen zur paulinischen Ekklesiologie," *TLZ* 102 [1977] 411–20. Worgul, G. S., "People of God, Body of Christ: Pauline Ecclesiological Contrasts," *BTB* 12 [1982] 24–28.)

128 (d) EUCHARIST. As mentioned above (→122), Paul uses "body of Christ" also to mean his eucharistic body. "As for the bread that we break, is it not a participation in the body of Christ?" (1 Cor 10:16). In the eucharistic body, Paul finds a source not only of the union of Christians with Christ but also of Christians among themselves. The earliest account of the institution of the eucharist in the NT is found in 1 Cor 11:23–25. Though it may be related in origin to the Lucan account (22:15–20) and differs somewhat from that of Mark (14:22–25) and Matt (26:26–29), it is an independent record of that institution, possibly derived from the liturgy of the Antiochene church. Paul passes it on as a tradition (→16 above). His account is not so much an eyewitness's report as a quotation of a liturgical recitation of what the "Lord" did at the Last Supper, even with its directive rubric, "Do this in memory of me" (1 Cor 11:24). Paul does not recount the event in and for itself, but he alludes to it in discussing other problems. He mentions this meal of the Lord as part of his criticism of the abuses that had crept into Corinthian community suppers associated with the eucharist (1 Cor 11) or in the course of his remarks on the eating of meat sacrificed to idols (1 Cor 10).

129   For Paul the eucharist is above all the "Lord's Supper" (1 Cor 11:20), the repast at which the new people of God eats its "spiritual food" and consumes its "spiritual drink" (1 Cor 10:3–4). In this act it manifests itself as the community of the "new covenant" (1 Cor 11:25; cf. Jer 31:31; Exod 24:8), as it shares in "the table of the Lord" (1 Cor 10:21; cf. Mal 1:7,12). The communion of this people denotes not only its union with Christ and with one another, but also a proclamation of the Christ-event itself and its eschatological character.

130   Three aspects in particular reveal Paul's understanding of the eucharist as the source of Christian unity. (1) It is the ritual act whereby Christ's presence with his people is concretized. Paul quotes, in effect, the rite of liturgical celebration and comments on its meaning in the immediate context (1 Cor 11:27–32): Christ's body and blood are identified with the bread and the wine so consumed by the community. Any "unworthy" sharing in that repast brings judgment on the Christian, for one would be "profaning the body and blood of the Lord" (11:27). Because the Lord is identified with such food, those who partake of it may not violate its sacred character and the Lord's presence by abuses of individualism, of disregard of the poor, or of idol worship. One cannot argue away the realism of the identity of Christ with the eucharistic food in Paul's teaching, even if Paul does not explain how this identity is achieved. Through this presence the eucharistic Christ alone *brings about* unity of believers in Paul's view.

131   (2) As a memorial and proclamation of Christ's sacrificial death, the eucharist is a rallying point. "As often as you eat this bread and drink this cup, you proclaim the death of the Lord until he comes" (1 Cor 11:26). The community is to do this "in memory of" him (11:24). The repetition of this ritual act, in which the Lord's body and blood are made present to nourish his people, becomes a solemn proclamation of the Christ-event itself (it is "the death of the Lord"—"for you") announcing to those who share in the meal the salvific effect of that death. A sacrificial aspect is proclaimed through reference to covenant blood (11:25): The eucharistic cup is the blood of the "new covenant" (Jer 31:31), an allusion to Moses' sealing of the covenant of old with the blood of sacrificed animals (Exod 24:8). This allusion invests the shedding of Christ's blood with an efficacy analogous to that of the sacrifice sealing the covenant of Sinai (cf. 1 Cor 10:14–21).

132 (3) There is also an eschatological aspect to the eucharist, for the proclamation of the Lord's death must continue "until he comes" (a reference to the Parousia). Thus only Christ in his risen, glorious status fully accomplishes the salvation of those who partake of the table of the Lord. From such a view of the eucharist undoubtedly comes the ancient acclamation *maranatha,* "Our Lord, come!" (1 Cor 16:22; → 53 above).

(Boismard, M.-E., "The Eucharist according to Saint Paul," *The Eucharist in the New Testament: A Symposium* [ed. J. Delorme; Baltimore, 1964] 123–39. Bornkamm, G., *Early Christian Experience* [→115 above] 123–60. Chenderlin, F., *"Do This as My Memorial"* [AnBib 99; Rome, 1982]. Delling, G., "Das Abendmahlsgeschehen nach Paulus," *KD* 10 [1964] 61–77. Hahn, F., *The Worship of the Early Church* [Phl, 1973]. Jeremias, J., *The Eucharistic Words of Jesus* [Phl, 1977] 101–5. Käsemann, E., "The Pauline Doctrine of the Lord's Supper," *ENTT*, 108–35. Kilmartin, E. J., *The Eucharist in the Primitive Church* [EC, 1965]. Marxsen, W., *The Lord's Supper as a Christological Problem* [FBBS 25; Phl, 1970]. Neuenzeit, P., *Das Herrenmahl* [SANT 1; Munich, 1960]. Reumann, J., *The Supper of the Lord* [Phl, 1985] 1–52. Schweizer, E., *The Lord's Supper according to the New Testament* [FBBS 18; Phl, 1967].)

133 (e) THE CHURCH. For all its rarity in the Gospels (Matt 16:18; 18:17), the word *ekklēsia* is found frequently in the Pauline corpus. In Acts it does not occur in the first four chapters and thereafter is found in the sense of "church" only once (5:11, in a Lucan comment) before the story of Paul begins (9:1); after that 21 times. In Paul's uncontested letters it is found 44 times (in the Deutero-Paulines, 15 times; in the Pastorals, three times). This situation seems to suggest that it took some time before early Christians became aware of their union in Christ as *ekklēsia.* The abundant use of the term in Paul's letters does not really contradict this. Incidentally, in the three accounts of Paul's conversion in Acts, where the heavenly voice says, "Saul, Saul, why are you persecuting me? I am Jesus whom you are persecuting" (9:4–5; 22:7–8; 26:14–15), the "church" is never explicitly mentioned. Consequently, one should hesitate to include as an element of Paul's experience near Damascus an awareness of the Christian community either as "church" or as "the body of Christ." Both of these are Pauline ways of conceiving the Christian community; they are not Lucan. Hence the "me" of 9:4; 22:7; and 26:14 is not to be associated with the body-of-Christ notion in Pauline theology.

134 The data in Paul's letters also reveal a certain development in his thinking about the "church." In 1 Thess, Paul uses *ekklēsia* both to designate a local church (1:1 [cf. 2 Thess 1:1]) and in the phrase "church of God" (1 Thess 2:14). In the first sense it denotes the unity of the Thessalonians developed from their common faith and worship; in the second it is given by Paul as a title of predilection to the primitive Judean communities. In the LXX, *ekklēsia* was used to translate Hebr *qāhāl*, the term given to the assembly of the Israelites, particularly in their desert wanderings. They were "the *ekklēsia* of the Lord" (Deut 23:2) or "the *ekklēsia* of the people of God" (Judg 20:2; cf. Acts 7:38). It also designated the Israelites in liturgical gatherings (1 Kgs 8:55; 1 Chr 29:10). However, Paul's expression *ekklēsia tou theou* is unique (except possibly for Neh 13:1, where Sinaiticus reads *Kyriou* against all other mss.); but its exact equivalent is found in QL (1QM 4:10, where "congregation of God" is to be inscribed on one of the standards to be borne into the eschatological war). Given such a Palestinian Jewish background for the phrase, it probably became an apt designation for the primitive communities of Judea, the first units formed in Christian history and peculiarly linked through their Jewish roots with the Israelite "congregation" of old.

135 In Paul's great letters the same double sense of *ekklēsia* is found again, designating both the local churches of Galatia, Judea, Macedonia, and Cenchreae (Gal 1:2,22; 2 Cor 8:1; Rom 16:1) and the primitive communities of Judea as "church of God" (1 Cor 11:16). The latter titular use, however, is now applied also to the church of Corinth (1 Cor 1:2; 2 Cor 1:1). According to L. Cerfaux (*ChTSP*, 113), this titular usage does not designate the "universal church" as manifested at Corinth, but is rather a Pauline way of flattering a church with which he has had such stormy relations, now that they are being smoothed out. He accords to the Corinthian community the title that he has previously used of the mother-churches of Palestine (cf. 1 Cor 10:32). But in this extension of the titular usage one also detects a broadening of Paul's understanding of *ekklēsia;* it is beginning to denote the Christian community as transcending local barriers. This is the seed of Paul's teaching about the universality of the church. Precisely in 1 Cor one detects the planting of this seed, for when Paul warns the Corinthians against submitting ordinary matters of dispute for settlement to the judgment of "people who are nothing in the church" (1 Cor 6:4), one can seriously query whether he means merely the local church. Similarly, in 1 Cor 14:5,12, Paul speaks of "doing the church some good." Per se, these could be references to the local community, but one senses in the term at least the beginnings of a more general sense (cf. 1 Cor 12:28). Strangely enough, in Rom, the letter often regarded as the most representative of Paul's theology, *ekklēsia* is absent, save for five instances in chap. 16, all of which refer to local churches (vv 1,4,5,16,23). Part of the problem is that this chapter in Rom has a character quite different from the rest of Rom, even if one admits that it is integral to the letter.

136 (In the Deutero-Paulines, *ekklēsia* plays an important role as a crucial part of the "mystery of Christ." The barrier between Jew and Greek has been broken down, and all human beings have been reconciled to God in Christ's "body, the church" [Col 1:17]. According to the view of Paul's disciple, the cosmic Christ is now the head of the church, which is his body; he is preeminent in all creation. For God "has put all things under his feet and made him the supreme head of the church, which is his body, the fullness of him who is filled out, all in all" [Eph 1:22–23]. In this passage the church is said to be "the fullness" [*plērōma*] of Christ; contrast Col 1:19; 2:9. It is given cosmic dimensions, and even the spirits, who are not members of the church, are said to learn about the Father's plan of salvific activity in Christ through the church [Eph 3:9–11]. Note the order in the praise given by Paul's disciple to the Father for his wisdom "through the church and through Christ Jesus" [Eph 3:21]—the church becomes so important that it seems to take precedence over Christ!)

137 For Paul himself, the "church" represents a development in his thinking about Christ's role in salvation. It is the concrete manifestation among human beings who have been baptized "in one Spirit to form one body" (1 Cor 12:13). The unity of these believers in one body, that is, the church that transcends all local barriers, is Paul's great contribution to Christian theology. It is a unity that is for him derived from the single purpose of the divine plan for the salvation of human beings in Christ Jesus. Paul came eventually to look on the "church of God" as a unit transcending both Jews and Greeks, yet incorporating them both when they became believers (1 Cor 10:32).

(Berger, K., "Volksversammlung und Gemeinde Gottes: Zu den Anfängen der christlichen Verwendung von 'ekklesia,'" *ZTK* 73 [1976] 167–207. Best, E., *One Body in Christ* [London, 1955]. Cerfaux, L., *ChTSP*. Coenen, L., "Church, Synagogue," *NIDNTT* 1, 291–307. Gärtner, B., *The Temple and the Community in Qumran and the New Testament* [SNTSMS 1; Cambridge, U.K., 1965]. Hainz, J., *Ekklesia: Strukturen paulinischer Gemeinde-Theologie und Gemeinde-Ordnung* [MTS 9: Regensburg, 1972]. Käsemann, E., *NTQT*, 252–59. Holmberg, B., *Paul and Power: The Structure of Authority in the Primitive Church as Reflected in the Pauline Epistles* [ConBNT 11; Lund, 1978]. Lanne, E., "L'Eglise une," *Irénikon* 50 [1977] 46–58. Minear, P. S., *Images of the Church in the New Testament* [2d ed.; Phl, 1975]. Pfammatter, J., *Die Kirche als Bau* [AnGreg 110; Rome, 1960]. Roloff, J., "Ekklesia," *EWNT* 1, 998–1011. Schlier, H., *Christus und die Kirche im Epheserbrief* [BHT 6; Tübingen, 1930]. Schmidt, K. L., "Ekklesia," *TDNT* 3, 501–36. Schnackenburg, R., *The Church in the New Testament* [NY, 1965]; "Ortsgemeinde und 'Kirche Gottes' im Ersten Korintherbrief," *Ortskirche Weltkirche* [Fest. J. Döpfner; Würzburg, 1973] 32–47. Schweizer, E., "Die Kirche als Leib Christi in den paulinischen Homologumena," *TLZ* 86 [1961] 161–74.)

138 (III) Paul's Ethics. (A) Dual Polarity of Christian Life. No sketch of Pauline theology would be adequate without a discussion of Paul's ethical teaching. For all his letters not only teach fundamental truths about the Christ-event (his christocentric soteriology) but also exhort Christians to upright ethical conduct. And it is not simply a matter of the hortatory sections of his letters, for exhortations are found elsewhere as well. There is, however, a certain tension between his theology and his ethics: Does it make a difference what justified, reconciled, or redeemed Christians do in their lives? On the one hand, Paul insists that Christians have become a "new creation" (Gal 6:15), in whom Christ really lives (Gal 2:20). We have already mentioned the integral Christian life that this elicits (→109). Christians have been justified by grace through faith in Christ Jesus (Rom 3:24–25) so that they are no longer "under law, but under grace" (Rom 6:15). On the other hand, even they still have to be delivered "from the present wicked world" (Gal 1:14; cf. 1 Cor 7:26,29–31). You must "not be conformed to this world, but be transformed by the renewal of your mental attitude so that you may assess the will of God—what is good, pleasing to him, and perfect" (Rom 12:2). Paul still tells the Christian who has experienced the effects of the Christ-event: "Work out your own salvation in fear and trembling" (Phil 2:12c); "for we must all appear before Christ's judgment-seat so that each one may receive good or evil for what one has done in the body" (2 Cor 5:10). Yet Paul knows that "God is the one working in you, both to will and to work for his good pleasure" (Phil 2:13; → 71). The Christian, then, lives a life of dual polarity.

139 The dual polarity that characterizes Christian life is the reason why Paul insists that the Christian energized by the Spirit of God (Rom 8:14) can no longer sin or live a life bound by a merely natural, earthly horizon. One is no longer *psychikos*, "material," but *pneumatikos*, "spiritual," one must fasten, then, one's gaze on the horizon of the Spirit that comes from God (1 Cor 2:11). Whereas the material person does not welcome what comes from the Spirit, the spiritual person is alive to everything, does not stifle the Spirit or disregard its promptings, but tests all things and holds on to what is good (1 Thess 5:19–22). This dual polarity also explains Christian freedom, in which Paul's Galatian converts are exhorted to stand firm (Gal 5:1): freedom from the law, freedom from sin and death, freedom from the self (Rom 6:7–11,14; 7:24–8:2). But that freedom is not an antinomian license. Paul vigorously rejects the idea that Christians should blatantly sin in order to give God more scope for his mercy and gracious justification (Rom 6:1; cf. 3:5–8). The "law of Christ" (Gal 6:2), when scrutinized, is seen to be a "law of love," explained in terms of bearing one another's burdens (in a context of fraternal correction). Even more explicitly, Paul repeats commandments 5, 6, 7, and 8 of the Decalogue, summing them up as, "You must love your neighbor as you do yourself" (Rom 13:8–10) and concluding, "So love fully satisfies the law." This is precisely "the law of the Spirit" (Rom 8:2), so that Christ has not simply substituted another legal code for the law of Moses. The "law of the

Spirit" may be a reflection of Jer 31:33, but it is more likely that Paul has coined the phrase to describe the Spirit's activity in terms of *nomos*, about which he has just been speaking. The Spirit's law of love is the new inner source and guide of the life by which the *pneumatikos* lives; it is the ontic principle of new vitality, whence springs the love that must interiorize the Christian's entire ethical conduct. And yet it is to such spiritual persons that Paul addresses his varied exhortations to virtuous conduct. We can only single out here a few of his characteristic exhortations, but before doing so we must say a few more words about the relation of Paul's ethics to his theology.

140 (B) Pauline Ethics and Pauline Theology. Patristic writers, medieval scholastics, and Reformation and Post-Tridentine theologians had often used Paul's ethical teachings in treatises on moral theology, but it was only in 1868 that H. Ernesti made the first attempt to synthesize Paul's ethics. (Part of the reason for the neglect of the latter stemmed from the way earlier theologians viewed the relation between revelation and natural law, between philosophical and Christian ethics.) Ernesti's starting point was that human beings were called to a status of righteousness before God, to an obedience to God's will, which is the absolute and unconditioned norm of Christian morality. He emphasized the freedom of the Christian in ethical conduct because of the gift of the Spirit. From the outset the study of Pauline ethics was dominated by vestiges of the Reformation debate about justification by faith and freedom from the law (see V. P. Furnish, *Theology and Ethics*, 242–79). In the early part of the present century, A. Schweitzer sought to free the discussion of Pauline ethics from the doctrine of justification and emphasized rather the eschatological aspect of such teaching. Paul's ethics have an interim, temporary character and are grounded in his "mysticism," that is, the Christian's share in the dying and rising of Christ. Being "in Christ," Christians are in possession of the Spirit, the life-principle of the new existence on which they have embarked. Later on (1924) R. Bultmann again related Paul's ethics to his doctrine of (forensic) justification by faith and introduced a distinction between the Pauline *indicative* (You are a justified Christian) and the Pauline *imperative* (Then live like a Christian): "*Because the Christian is freed from sin through justification, he ought to wage war against sin.*" Yet the righteousness of the Christian is an eschatological phenomenon, for it does not depend on human accomplishment, moral or otherwise, but solely on the event of God's grace, an otherworldly phenomenon. This righteousness is not an "ethical" quality; it involves no change in the moral character of a human being. Faith is obedience, and human ethical acts do not bring about righteousness; rather, they are the expressions of the radical obedience to which humans are called. Still later, C. H. Dodd (1927) introduced the distinction between *kērygma* and *didachē*, which roughly corresponded for him to "theology" and "ethics," or to "gospel" and "law." A new age has dawned (realized eschatology), and Paul is the promulgator of its new law, a Christian pattern for conduct to which a Christian is obliged to conform, "the law of Christ" (Gal 6:2). Reverting to an emphasis of A. Schweitzer, of H. D. Wendland, and of others, V. P. Furnish (1968) considered eschatology to be "the heuristic key" to Pauline theology, the lever to organize the other elements in his teaching, including the ethical. His understanding of Pauline eschatology differs from Schweitzer's and is nuanced enough to be acceptable (→ 47 above), and certainly eschatology is important in Pauline ethics (see Phil 2:12; 2 Cor 5:10; Rom 2:6–11). Yet it is not the heuristic key to the whole (see my review, *JPST* 22 [1969] 113–15). The best way to explain the relation of Paul's ethics to his theology, in my opinion, is to see the former as a detailed, concrete explanation of the love that is the way for Christian faith to work itself out. In other words, Gal 5:6 ("faith working itself out through love") again proves its importance in Pauline thinking, for it is the link between Pauline theology and ethics.

(Austgen, R. J., *Natural Motivation in the Pauline Epistles* [2d ed.; Notre Dame, IN, 1969]. Bultmann, R., "Das Problem der Ethik bei Paulus," *ZNW* 23 [1924] 123–40; *Exegetica* [Tübingen, 1967] 36–54. Corriveau, R., *The Liturgy of Life: A Study of the Ethical Thought of St. Paul in His Letters to the Early Christian Communities* [Montreal, 1970]. Enslin, M. S., *The Ethics of Paul* [Nash, 1957]. Ernesti, H., *Die Ethik des Apostels Paulus in ihren Grundzügen dargestellt* [Göttingen, 1868]. Furnish, V. P., *Theology and Ethics in Paul* [Nash, 1968]. Glaser, J. W., "Commands—Counsels: A Pauline Teaching?" *TS* 31 [1970] 275–87. Gnilka, J., "Paränetische Traditionen im Epheserbrief," *Mélanges bibliques en hommage au R. P. Béda Rigaux* [eds. A. Descamps and A. de Halleux; Gembloux, 1970] 397–410. Hasenstab, R., *Modelle paulinischer Ethik* [Tübinger theologische Studien 11; Mainz, 1977]. Merk, O., *Handeln aus Glauben: Die Motivierungen der paulinischen Ethik* [MarThSt 5; Marburg, 1968]. Moule, C. F. D., "Obligation in the Ethic of Paul," *Christian History and Interpretation* [Fest J. Knox; eds. W. R. Farmer and others; Cambridge, U.K., 1967] 389–406. Romaniuk, K., "Les motifs parénétiques dans les écrits pauliniens," *NovT* 10 [1968] 191–207. Schnackenburg, R., *The Moral Teaching of the New Testament* [NY, 1965] 261–306. Strecker, G., "Ziele und Ergebnisse einer neutestamentlichen Ethik," *NTS* 25 [1978–79] 1–15. Watson, N. M., "Justified by Faith; Judged by Works—An Antinomy?" *NTS* 29 [1983] 209–21. Westerholm, S., "Letter and Spirit: The Foundation of Pauline Ethics," *NTS* 30 [1984] 229–48.)

141   (C) Christian Life and Its Demands. Paul's ethical teaching, in its specific and concrete recommendations, echoes at once his Pharisaic, Jewish background (→10–11) and his Hellenistic background (→12). When Paul exhorts his readers to proper Christian conduct, his recommendations fall under various headings. Some, which have been analyzed form-critically, are the generic ethical lists of virtues and vices (and *Haustafeln*). Others are more specific.

142 (a) ETHICAL LISTS. In his uncontested letters, Paul incorporates catalogues of virtues and vices that should or should not characterize Christian life (Gal 5:19–23; 1 Cor 5:10–11; 6:9–10; 2 Cor 6:6–7; 12:20; Rom 1:29–31; 13:13 [Col 3:5–8,12–14; Eph 5:3–5]). The eschatological reference in these catalogues is often evident: "People who do such things will not inherit the kingdom of God" (Gal 5:21). Because "kingdom of God" is hardly an operative element in Pauline teaching (occurring elsewhere only in 1 Thess 2:12; 1 Cor 4:20; 6:9–10; 15:24,50; Rom 14:17), the association of it with these catalogues seems to mark them as elements of pre-Pauline catechetical instruction, which he has inherited and made use of. These lists have been compared with similar ones found in Hellenistic (especially Stoic) philosophical writings and in Palestinian Jewish texts (e.g., of the Essenes; cf. 1QS 4:2–6,9–11).

(Easton, B. S., "New Testament Ethical Lists," *JBL* 51 [1932] 1–12. Kamlah, E., *Die Form der katalogischen Paränese im Neuen Testament* [WUNT 7; Tübingen, 1964]. Segalla, G., "I cataloghi dei peccati in S. Paolo," *SPat* 15 [1968] 205–28. Vögtle, A., *Die Tugend- und Lasterkataloge im Neuen Testament* [NTAbh 16/4–5; Münster, 1936]. Wibbing, S., *Die Tugend- und Lasterkataloge im Neuen Testament und ihre Traditionsgeschichte unter besonderer Berücksichtigung der Qumran-Texte* [BZNW 25; Berlin, 1959].)

143 (In the Deutero-Paulines [Col 3:18–4:1; Eph 5:21–6:9] and in the Pastoral Letters [1 Tim 2:8–15; Titus 2:1–10] one finds another literary list, the so-called *Haustafel* [a term from Luther's *Deutsche Bibel* that has become a standard designation even in English]. Roughly, it would mean a "domestic bulletin board," for it lists the Christian obligations or duties and chores of members of the household, i.e., the *familia* of the Greco-Roman world: husband and wives, parents and children, and masters and slaves. These lists show a Pauline disciple coping with social ethical problems of his day, but they list little more than generalities.)

(Crouch, J. E., *The Origin and Intention of the Colossian Haustafel* [FRLANT 109; Göttingen, 1973]. Schrage, W., "Zur Ethik der neutestamentlichen Haustafeln," *NTS* 21 [1974–75] 1–22. Weidinger, K., *Die Haustafeln: Ein Stück urchristlicher Paränese* [UNT 14; Leipzig, 1928].)

144 (b) CONSCIENCE. We might well have included this element of Paul's teaching under "Human Beings" above (→101–7), but we prefer to treat it here because of the relation to his ethics. "Conscience" is the capacity to judge one's actions either in retrospect (as right or wrong) or in prospect (as a guide for proper activity). Paul's word for it is *syneidēsis* (= Lat *con-scientia*). It is related to *nous*, "mind" (Rom 7:23,25), but is best treated separately. It has no counterpart in the OT or in QL, but enters the Judaic tradition in the LXX (Job 27:6; Qoh 10:20; cf. Sir 42:18; Wis 17:10). The claim that it was derived by Paul from Stoic philosophy is debatable; more likely it is from the popular Hellenistic philosophy of his day. Initially, *syneidēsis* denoted "consciousness" (of human activity in general); eventually it was applied to consciousness of moral aspects, at first as "bad conscience," then as "conscience" in general. Of the 30 NT occurrences, 14 are found in 1 and 2 Cor and Rom (and six in the Pastorals): 1 Cor 8:7,10,12; 10:25,27,28,29bis; 2 Cor 1:12; 4:2; 5:11; Rom 2:15; 9:1; 13:5. Three passages are particularly important: (1) Rom 2:14–15, where Paul recognizes that by means of "conscience" Gentiles perform some of the prescriptions of the Mosaic law and are thus a "law" unto themselves. (2) 1 Cor 8:7–12, where Paul calls upon the Christian to respect the weak conscience of a fellow Christian troubled about eating food consecrated to idols. (3) 1 Cor 10:23–29, where Paul discusses a similar problem. In 2 Cor 1:12, Paul relates the conscience to the problem of boasting; in Rom 8:16; 9:1, he relates it to the gift of the Spirit. Paul's teaching on the subject has often been compared to that in later rabbinic texts about the *yēṣer hārāᶜ* and *yēṣer haṭṭôb*, "evil impulse" and "good impulse."

(Coune, M., "Le problème des idolothytes et l'éducation de la syneidêsis," *RSR* 51 [1963] 497–534. Davies, W. D., "Conscience," *IDB* 1, 671–76. Jewett, R., *Paul's Anthropological Terms* [AGJU 10; Leiden, 1971] 402–46. Maurer, C., "*Synoida, Syneidēsis*", *TDNT* 7, 899–919. Pierce, C. A., *Conscience in the New Testament* [SBT 15; London, 1955]. Stelzenberger, J., *Syneidesis im Neuen Testament* [Abh. z. Moraltheologie 1; Paderborn, 1961]. Stendahl, K., "The Apostle Paul and the Introspective Conscience of the West," *HTR* 56 [1963] 199–215. Therrien, G., *Le discernement dans les écrits pauliniens* [EBib; Paris, 1973] 263–301. Thrall, M. E., "The Pauline Use of *syneidēsis*," *NTS* 14 [1967–68] 118–25.)

145 (c) NATURAL LAW. Related to the question of "conscience" in Paul's teaching is that of the so-called natural law. Because it is a debated issue, we have not included it above (→ 89–100), since Paul's view of the law of Moses is complicated enough. Moreover, Pauline teaching that bears on this issue is better related to his ethics. The issue arises mainly because of Rom 2:14–15, "When Gentiles who do not have the law do by nature [*physei*] what the law prescribes, they are a law [*nomos*] to themselves, even though they do not have the law. They show that the deed prescribed by the law is written on their hearts, while their conscience also bears witness and their conflicting thoughts accuse or perhaps excuse them." The *nomos* of v 14 has been related to the "another law" or to "the law of my mind" in Rom 7:23, probably wrongly, for the prime analogate there is the Mosaic law. In Rom 2:14 we have one of the figurative uses of *nomos* (→ 90). Although in 1 Cor 11:14, Paul does argue from "nature" (*physis*), in Rom 2:14 he may merely be quoting a contention of others (perhaps one should set quotation marks about "by nature" in Rom 2:14). Also, in speaking of a law written on the heart, Paul may only be echoing Jer 31:33 or Isa 51:7. Thus, it is difficult to be certain about his views of the "natural law," an idea more at home in Gk philosophy. Perhaps the most that should be admitted is that the idea be regarded as the *sensus plenior* of Paul's teaching (in view of the patristic tradition about it).

(Dodd, C. H., "Natural Law in the New Testament, *New Testament Studies* [Manchester, U.K., 1953] 129–42. Flückiger, F., "Die Werke des Gesetzes bei den Heiden (nach Röm. 2,14 ff.)," *TZ* 8 [1952] 17–42. Greenwood, D., "St. Paul and Natural Law," *BTB* 1 [1971] 262–79. Lyonnet, S., "Lex naturalis et iustificatio gentilium," *VD* 41 [1963] 238–42. McKenzie, J. L., "Natural Law in the New Testament," *BR* 9 [1964] 1–13.)

146 (d) PRAYER AND ASCETICISM. These are prime considerations of Christian life, because one sees Paul himself not only engaged in them, but also speaking about them in a reflex manner. For Paul "prayer" is the explicit recollection of the Christian that one lives in the presence of God and has the duty of communing with him in adoration, praise, thanksgiving, and supplication. Paul's letters are permeated with expressions of prayer; the formal thanksgiving in each letter, except Gal and 2 Cor, is an integral part of his writing—and not merely conformity with an epistolary custom. The object of his prayer is at times himself (1 Thess 3:11; 2 Cor 12:8–9), his converts (1 Thess 3:9–10,12–13; Phil 1:9–11; 2 Cor 13:7–9), or his former co-religionists, the Jewish people (Rom 10:1). Paul often exhorts his readers to pray (1 Thess 5:16–18; Phil 4:6; Rom 12:11–12); it is the mark of the mature Christian disciple, who prays to God as Abba (Gal 4:1–6). The ground of Christian prayer is the Spirit (Rom 8:15–16,26–27), who aids Christians in praying, interceding on their behalf (8:28–30). Paul prays to the Father (*theos*) through Christ and in the Spirit (Rom 1:8; 7:25). Examples of his prayers: doxologies (2 Cor 11:31; Phil 4:21; Rom 1:25; 11:33–36; [Eph 3:20–21]); intercessory petitions (1 Thess 3:11–13; 5:23–24); benedictional confessions (2 Cor 1:3–7; [Eph 1:3–14]); thanksgivings (1 Thess 1:3–4; Phil 1:3–11; 1 Cor 1:4–9; Rom 1:8–12). Paul could even consider his preaching of the gospel a form of worship (Rom 15:16–17).

Linked to such prayer and worship is Paul's ascetical attitude. Though he never speaks of *askēsis*, he does regard *enkrateia*, "self-control, self-discipline," as a fruit of the Spirit (Gal 5:23). This attitude is owing not simply to the imminence of the Parousia (1 Cor 7:29–31), but to his view of life as a struggle (1 Thess 5:6–8; 2 Cor 10:3–4; 4:7–11 [suffering as a passive asceticism]), or as an athletic competition (Phil 3:12–14; 1 Cor 9:24–27, where the asceticism is active). Paul freely renounced his right to recompense for preaching the gospel (1 Cor 9:1,4–18) lest he be tempted to boast. Specific forms of asceticism are recommended by him: the use of material abundance to help those in need (2 Cor 8:8–15); temporary abstinence from the marital act "to devote oneself to prayer" (1 Cor 7:5–6).

(Campenhausen, H. von, "Early Christian Asceticism," *Tradition and Life in the Church* [Phl, 1968] 90–122. Cerfaux, L., "L'Apôtre en présence de Dieu: Essai sur la vie d'oraison de saint Paul," *Recueil* 2, 469–81. Giardini, F., "Conversione, ascesi e mortificazione nelle lettere di S. Paolo," *RAM* 12 [1967] 197–225. Niederwimmer, K., "Zur Analyse der asketischen Motivation in 1. Kor. 7," *TLZ* 99 [1974] 241–48. Quinn, J., "Apostolic Ministry and Apostolic Prayer," *CBQ* 33 [1971] 479–91. Stanley, D. M., *Boasting in the Lord* [NY, 1973]. Wiles, G. P., *Paul's Intercessory Prayers* [SNTSMS 24; Cambridge, U.K., 1974].)

147 (e) MARRIAGE, CELIBACY, AND WIDOWHOOD. Paul considers marriage, celibacy (or virginity), and widowhood, along with slavery and civic freedom, as conditions of life in which Christians find themselves. The principle that governs his view of them is expressed in 1 Cor 7:17, "Let each one walk in the lot that the Lord has assigned to him and in which God has called him." 1 Cor 7 spells out various details of such ways of life. For Paul, both marriage and celibacy are God-given charisms (7:7b). He recommends monogamous marriage, with its mutual rights and obligations, because "there is so much immorality" (*dia tas porneias*, 7:2) and because "it is better to marry than to burn with passion" (7:9b). But Paul clearly recognizes the salvific character of marriage, the influence of one spouse on the other and on the children born of them (7:12,14–16), even when the marriage involves a Christian and a non-Christian. He repeats as a charge "from the Lord" the absolute prohibition of divorce (and subsequent remarriage, 7:10–11). But in saying that "the wife should not separate from her husband," Paul's formulation is already adapted to a Greco-Roman setting, where divorce instituted by a woman was possible (cf. the Palestinian setting in the formulation of Luke 16:18). But when the marriage is "mixed" (i.e., between a Christian and a non-Christian), Paul—not the Lord—tolerates separation or divorce, if the two cannot live in peace (7:15), whence develops later the so-called Pauline privilege. In 1 Cor 7, Paul never tries to justify marriage in terms of a purpose of procreation; nor does he show any concern there for the Christian family. (This will be remedied by the *Haustafeln* of the Deutero-Paulines.) Paul echoes the contemporary view of women in the society of his day when he speaks of the "husband" as "the head of the wife" (1 Cor 11:3; see further 11:7–12; 14:34–35 [probably a non-Pauline interpolation!]). But one has to recall that the same Paul writes in Gal 3:28, "There is neither Jew nor Greek, neither slave nor free, neither male or female, for you are all one in Christ Jesus."

(One finds in Eph 5:21–33 a different, and somewhat more exalted, view of Christian marriage. The author begins by asserting the mutual subjection of all "out of reverence for Christ." Then he immediately says, "Wives, be subject to your husbands, as to the Lord" [5:22]—a subordinate role of wives, echoing 1 Cor 11:3, that is tempered by the instruction to husbands, "Love your wives" [5:25]. Here the author is trying to cope with the psychological difference between husbands and wives, as he insists on the mutual obligation that they both have to each other. But he does it in the only—time-conditioned—way that he knows: The wife must be subject, and the husband must love. He never implies that the wife is an inferior being. As a model for the husband's love, he cites the love of Christ for the church [5:25]. Finally, in quoting Gen 2:24, "For this reason a man leaves father and mother and clings to his wife, and the two become one flesh," the author reveals a "secret" [*mystērion*] hidden in that verse of Gen centuries before, that is, that the fundamental union of marriage established by God long ago was a prefigured "type" of the union of Christ and his church. This view of the sublimity of marriage has colored much of the Christian tradition throughout the centuries.)

148 As for celibacy, Paul states his preference gradually in 1 Cor 7. Celibacy is his own opinion, "not a command of the Lord" (7:25), even though he thinks that he is as attuned to the Spirit in this matter as anyone else (7:40). At first, there is no comparison, "It is good for a man not to touch a woman" (7:1), but his preference emerges in 7:7a, "I wish that all were as I myself am." Again, "to the unmarried and the widows I say, It is good for them to remain as I am" (7:8)—an unclear statement usually understood as meaning that Paul aligns himself with the "unmarried" (but → Paul, 19). Paul gives two reasons for his preference: (1) "because of the impending distress" (7:26, i.e., the imminent Parousia; cf. 7:29; 1 Thess 4:15,17; Rom 13:11); and (2) because one is thus freed from "worldly cares" (7:28) and "divided interests" (i.e., the concern for a husband or a wife) so that one can give "undivided devotion to the Lord" (7:32–35). Here a comparison between the married and the unmarried is implied, and Paul recommends celibacy in view of apostolic service. At the end of the chapter he introduces the comparison explicitly in the difficult passage about the marrying of one's "virgin" (daughter, ward, fiancée?): "The man who marries her does what is right, but he who does not does even better" (*kreisson poiēsei*, 7:38). As for widows, Paul recognizes their right to marry again, but he judges that they will be happier if they remain widows.

(Allmen, J. J. von, *Pauline Teaching on Marriage* [London, 1963]. Baltensweiler, H., *Die Ehe im Neuen Testament* [Zürich, 1967]. Crouzel, H., *L'Eglise primitive face au divorce* [Théologie historique 13; Paris, 1971]. Dulau, P., "The Pauline Privilege," *CBQ* 13 [1951] 146–52. Elliott, J. K., "Paul's Teaching on Marriage in I Corinthians," *NTS* 19 [1972–73] 219–25. Greeven, H., "Ehe nach dem Neuen Testament," *NTS* 15 [1968–69] 365–88. Grelot, P., *Man and Wife in Scripture* [NY, 1964]. Matura, T., "Le célibat dans le Nouveau Testament d'après l'exégèse récente," *NRT* 107 [1975] 593–604. Niederwimmer, K., "*Gameō*, etc.," *EWNT* 1, 564–71. Pesch, R., *Freie Treue; Die Christen und die Ehescheidung* [Freiburg, 1971]. Swain, L., "Paul on Celibacy," *ClR* 51 [1966] 785–91.)

149 (f) SOCIETY, STATE, AND SLAVERY. Paul recognizes differences both in human and in Christian society. He recognizes that both Jews and Greeks have been called to become children of God through faith and baptism and their oneness in the church, the body of Christ. Though he does not obliterate all distinctions, he recognizes their lack of value in Christ Jesus. "By one Spirit we were all baptized into one body, Jews or Greeks, slaves or free; and all were made to drink of the same Spirit" (1 Cor 12:13; cf. Gal 3:28). Yet he can also say, "Let each one walk in the lot to which the Lord has assigned him . . . ; everyone should remain in the state in which one was called" (1 Cor 7:17–20). For Paul's basic attitude is expressed in 1 Cor 9:19–23: "I have become all things to all that I may save some." Hence he reckons with Jews and Greeks, slaves and free, men and women, rich and poor, married and celibate, the weak in conviction and the strong, the material and the spiritual ones in Christian society.

150 Paul is also aware that the Christian must live in civil and political society that is not wholly oriented to the same goals as the Christian community. Christians may in reality be citizens of another, a heavenly "commonwealth" (Phil 3:20), but they do have obligations of another sort in this earthly life. These Paul treats in Rom 13:1–7, and indirectly in 1 Cor 6:1–8; 2:6–8. One can agree with E. Käsemann that Paul does not really have an "ethic" of the state ("Principles," 196), or even a well-formulated systematic understanding of it. Rom 13:1–7 has been suspected of being an interpolation, but it stands today as part of the hortatory section of that letter. In it Paul recognizes that Christians must subject themselves to the "authorities," who are most likely human state officials, even though some have tried to identify them as angelic beings. Christians are to recognize their place in the structure of human society. Paul's motivating reasons are mainly three: (1) eschatological (the danger of facing "judgment" [13:2] and "wrath" [13:5]); (2) the dictate of "conscience" itself (13:5); and (3) "the [common] good" (13:4). For the same reasons Paul insists that Christians must not only "pay taxes" and "revenue" (13:6–7a), but accord the authorities "honor" and "respect" (13:7b). Underlying Paul's discussion is the conviction that "there is no authority except from God and those that exist have been set up by God" (13:1). In writing to the Romans, Paul is implicitly recognizing the God-given character of the authority of the Roman empire in which he himself was living. The trouble with his teaching in this passage is that he never envisages the possibility that human authorities could be evil or could do evil; it does no good to try to save Paul in this matter by invoking angelic authorities. His teaching is limited; and even his reference to "the [common] good" (13:4a) can scarcely be invoked in defense of civil disobedience.

151 Lastly, Paul's counsel to slaves in 1 Cor 7:21–22 is always a difficult teaching to cope with. Paul did not seek to change the social system in which he lived. This is undoubtedly the reason why he returns the runaway slave Onesimus to his master Philemon (Phlm 8–20). Yet in the latter passage we may detect what he really thinks about the matter; for he sends Onesimus back as "more than a slave," as a "brother" (16), i.e., suggesting that Philemon recognize him as a fellow Christian, and possibly even hinting that he should emancipate him (though the latter is far from certain). Paul was in this instance more concerned about interiorizing the existing social situation than in changing it, realizing that even a slave in civil society could have freedom in Christ Jesus (Gal 3:28). (Cf. Col 3:22–4:1; Eph 6:5–9.)

(Bartchy, S. S., *Mallon chrēsai* [→ 75 above]. Borg, M., "A New Context for Romans xiii," *NTS* 19 [1972–73] 205–18. Broer, I., *"Exousia," EWNT* 2, 23–29. Coleman-Norton, P. R., "The Apostle Paul and the Roman Law of Slavery," *Studies in Roman Economic and Social History* [Princeton, N.J., 1951] 155–77. Cook, W. R., "Biblical Light on the Christian's Civil Responsibility," *BSac* 127 [1970] 44–57. Cullmann, O., *The State in the New Testament* [NY, 1956]. Hutchinson, S., "The Political Implications of Romans 13:1–7," *Biblical Theology* 21 [1971] 49–59. Käsemann, E., "Principles of the Interpretation of Romans 13," *NTQT*, 196–216. Lyall, F., "Roman Law in the Writings of Paul—The Slave and the Freedman," *NTS* 17 [1970–71] 73–79. Murphy-O'Connor, J., "The Christian and Society in St. Paul," *New Blackfriars* 50 [1968–69] 174–82. Pagels, E. H., "Paul and Women: A Response to Recent Discussion," *JAAR* 42 [1974] 538–49. Scroggs, R., "Paul and the Eschatological Woman," *JAAR* 40 [1972] 283–301; cf. *JAAR* 42 [1974] 432–37.)

Conclusion

152 Paul has instructions for Christian conduct in other areas as well, which cannot be included in this brief sketch. We conclude our remarks on Paul's theology and ethics by insisting on its christocentrism. As Christ was "the image of God" (2 Cor 4:4), so human beings are destined to be "the image of the heavenly man" (1 Cor 15:49; cf. Rom 8:29). It is growth in Christ that Paul recommends to his readers, both contemporary and modern. In this way the Christian lives his or her life "for God" (Gal 2:19). Thus, for all his emphasis on Christ, Paul once again refers Christian existence ultimately to the Father—through Christ.

GENERAL BIBLIOGRAPHY

BARRETT, C. K., *Essays on Paul* (Phl, 1982).

BEKER, J. C., *Paul the Apostle: The Triumph of God in Life and Thought* (Phl, 1980).

——, *Paul's Apocalyptic Gospel: The Coming Triumph of God* (Phl, 1982).

BORNKAMM, G., *Paul* (NY, 1971).

BROWN, R. E., *The Churches the Apostles Left Behind* (NY, 1984).

BROWN, R. E. and J. P. MEIER, *Antioch and Rome* (NY, 1982).

BROX, N., *Understanding the Message of Paul* (Notre Dame, IN, 1968).

BRUCE, F. F., *Paul, Apostle of the Heart Set Free* (Exeter, U.K., 1977).

BULTMANN, R., *TNT* 1, 185–352.

CADBURY, H. J., *The Book of Acts in History* (London, 1955) 123–33.

CAMPFELL, T. H., "Paul's 'Missionary Journeys' as Reflected in His Letters," *JBL* 74 (1955) 80–87.

DEISSMANN, A., *St. Paul, a Study in Social and Religious History* (London, 1912; repr., Magnolia, MA, 1972).

DOCKX, S. "Chronologie de la vie de Saint Paul, depuis sa conversion jusqu'à son séjour à Rome," *NovT* 13 (1971) 261–304.

——, *Chronologies néotestamentaires et vie de l'église primitive* (Gembloux, 1976) 45–128.

DODD, C. H., *The Meaning of Paul for Today* (NY, 1972).

DRANE, J. W., *Paul, Libertine or Legalist?* (London, 1975).

GIBLIN, C. H., *In Hope of God's Glory* (NY, 1970).

GUNTHER, J. J., *Paul: Messenger and Exile* (Valley Forge, PA, 1972).

HANSON, A. T., *Studies in Paul's Technique and Theology* (London, 1974).

HENGEL, M., *Acts and the History of Earliest Christianity* (Phl, 1979).

HURD, J. C., "Pauline Chronology and Pauline Theology," *Christian History and Interpretation* (Fest. J. Knox; ed. W. R. Farmer and others; Cambridge, U.K., 1976) 225–48.

——, "Paul the Apostle," *IDBSup* 648–51.

——, "The Sequence of Paul's Letters," *CJT* 14 (1968) 189–200.

JEWETT, R., *A Chronology of Paul's Life* (Phl, 1979).

KÄSEMANN, E., *Perspectives on Paul* (Phl, 1971).

KNOX, J., *Chapters in a Life of Paul* (NY 1950).

——, " 'Fourteen Years Later': A Note on the Pauline Chronology," *JR* 16 (1936) 341–49.

——, "The Pauline Chronology," *JBL* 58 (1939) 15–39.

KUSS, O., *Paulus: Die Rolle des Apostels in der theologischen Entwicklung der Urkirche* (Regensburg, 1971).

LONGENECKER, R. N., *Paul: Apostle of Liberty* (NY, 1964).

LÜDEMANN, G., *Paul, Apostle to the Gentiles: Studies in Chronology* (Phl, 1984).

LYONNET, S. and L. SABOURIN, *Sin, Redemption, and Sacrifice* (AnBib 48; Rome, 1970).

MARROW, S. B., *Paul: His Letters and His Theology* (NY, 1986).

MEEKS, W. A., *The First Urban Christians: The Social World of the Apostle Paul* (New Haven, CT, 1983).

——, *The Writings of St. Paul* (NY, 1972).

MURPHY-O'CONNOR, J., "Pauline Missions before the Jerusalem Conference," *RB* 89 (1982) 71–91.

——, *St. Paul's Corinth: Texts and Archaeology* (Wilmington, DE, 1983).

OGG, G., *The Chronology of the Life of Paul* (London, 1968).

RENGSTORF, K. H. (ed.), *Das Paulusbild in der neueren deutschen Forschung* (WF 24; 2d ed.; Darmstadt, 1969).

RIDDERBOS, H. N., *Paul: An Outline of His Theology* (GR, 1975).

RIDDLE, D. W., *Paul, Man of Conflict* (Nash, 1940).

RIGAUX, B., *The Letters of St. Paul* (Chicago, 1968).

SANDMEL, S., *The Genius of Paul* (Phl, 1979).

SCHOEPS, H. J., *Paul* (Phl, 1961).

SCHÜTZ, J. H., *Paul and the Anatomy of Apostolic Authority* (SNTSMS 26; Cambridge, U.K., 1975).

SHERWIN-WHITE, A. N., *Roman Society and Roman Law in the New Testament* (Oxford, U.K., 1969).

SMYTH, B. T., *Paul: Mystic and Missionary* (Maryknoll, NY, 1980).

STENDAHL, K., *Paul among Jews and Gentiles and Other Essays* (Phl, 1976).

SUHL, A., *Paulus und seine Briefe* (SNT 11; Gütersloh, 1975).

TAYLOR, M. J. (ed.), *A Companion to Paul: Readings in Pauline Theology* (Staten Island, NY, 1975).

WHITELEY, D. E. H., *The Theology of St. Paul* (2d ed.; Oxford, U.K., 1974).

INDEXES

The numbers refer to the boldface marginal numerals in the text of the book. Those preceded by P are found in Part One (Paul); those preceded by PT are found in Part Two (Pauline Theology). The notation GB refers to the modern authors listed in the General Bibliography on pp. 109–10.

Index of Modern Authors

)

Index of Subjects

Fair Havens, P 48
Faith, PT 6–7, 13, 21, 25–26, 31, 33, 42, 46,
    64, 68–69, 71, 95–98, 108–12, 116, 119,
    122, 125, 138, 140, 149
Famine visit, P 11, 25, 27
Felix, Antonius, Procurator, P 12, 47
Festus, Porcius, Procurator, P 6, 23, 48
Flesh, PT 76, 95–96, 101–3, 107, 111, 119,
    123, 147
    and spirit, PT 12, 24, 139
Forgiveness of sins, PT 75
Freedom, PT 12, 25, 36, 44, 67, 76, 111,
    139–40

Galatia
    North, P 6, 29, 38, 40, 44; PT 135
    South, P 6, 29, 30, 38, 44; PT 135
Gallio, L. Junius, P 5, 9, 39
Gamaliel I, the Elder, P 18
Gentile Christians, P 30, 34, 37; PT 43, 72
Gentiles (Greeks), P 20, 29–30, 32; PT 21, 28,
    43, 86–87, 114, 125, 136–37, 147, 149
Glorification, PT 45, 67, 80
Glory, PT 31, 43, 45, 47, 59, 76, 78, 82, 84–85,
    92, 107, 120
Gnosticism, gnostics, PT 12, 22
God (the Father), PT 10, 13–14, 21, 31,
    37–40, 45, 50, 59–60, 64, 72, 83–84,
    86–87, 94, 111, 115, 125, 138, 146, 150
    creator, PT 37, 78, 80
    fidelity of, PT 39
    love of, PT 40, 96
    predestination by, PT 41
    purpose of, PT 41
    steadfast mercy of, PT 39
    uprightness of, PT 39–40, 68, 70
    will of, PT 41, 87, 94
    wrath of, PT 38, 60, 87, 93, 150
Gospel, P 21, 32, 34, 39; PT 10, 15–16, 18, 21,
    30–37, 48, 71, 89, 109, 146
Grace, PT 21, 25, 43, 65–66, 69, 71, 97, 113,
    138
Greece, P 28, 51
Greeks, see Gentiles

Hagar, PT 76
Haustafel, PT 141, 143, 147
Heart, PT 101, 106
"Hebrews," PT 53
Hebrews, Epistle to the, PT 8
Hellenists, P 26–27; PT 53
Herodotus, PT 77
Holy of Holies, PT 73
Homer, PT 78

Hope, PT 64, 71
Hymns, PT 16, 111

Iconium, P 30
Illyricum, P 6, 43
Irenaeus, PT 32
Isis, PT 53
Israel, PT 14, 21, 43, 46, 48, 73, 90, 92, 97, 114
Italy, P 10, 48

James of Jerusalem, P 26, 32, 34–37, 47
Jerome, P 3
Jerusalem, P 6, 18, 20, 24–27, 31–33, 35–36,
    39, 41, 44–45, 47, 50; PT 19
Jesus of Nazareth, P 18, 23; PT 9, 14, 17–19,
    25, 32, 67, 121
    betrayal of, PT 19
    burial of, PT 19, 67, 113
    crucifixion of, PT 14, 19, 28–29, 33
    death of, PT 9, 14, 18, 25, 54–57, 67–68, 75,
        98, 113, 120, 131–32
    exaltation of, PT 59, 67
    heavenly intercession of, PT 67
    ministry of, PT 18
    passion of, PT 9, 18, 55, 67–68, 75, 120
    resurrection of, PT 9, 13–14, 18–19, 25, 35,
        50, 58–60, 67, 96, 98–99, 113
    sayings of, PT 18, 56, 113
    (see also Christ)
Jewish Christians, P 10, 30, 32, 47; PT 43,
    53–54, 72
Jews, PT 21, 28, 51–52, 54, 86–87, 114, 125,
    136–37, 146–47, 149
    expelled from Rome, P 10
John, son of Zebedee, P 32
Josephus, Flavius, P 10–12; PT 52, 68, 72
Judah, the Prince, Rabbi, PT 11
Judaizers, PT 21, 36, 69, 71, 76, 90
Judas Barsabbas, P 37
Judea, P 6, 12, 23, 25–26, 31; PT 134–35
Judgment, PT 45, 47, 68, 130, 150
Julius Alexander, T., P 11
Julius Caesar, P 17
Justification, PT 21, 24, 42, 44, 58, 60, 66–71,
    78, 80, 95–96, 111, 138–40

Kerygma, PT 3, 16, 25, 28, 36–37, 57, 140
Kingdom, PT 45, 80, 142

Lasea, P 48
Law
    Mosaic, P 30, 36, 47; PT 9–10, 14, 19, 21,
        25, 42–43, 46, 66, 68, 76, 86–87,
        89–101, 111, 113, 119, 138–40, 144–45
    natural, PT 145